FULLY EXPRESSED

Published by Pitch Club Publishing
Cover Design by Jen Rae

979-8-9892901-1-6 (KINDLE)
979-8-9892901-3-0 (PAPERBACK)

FULLY EXPRESSED

COMPILED BY
REBECCA CAFIERO

TWELVE WOMEN.
A KALEIDOSCOPE OF TRUTH.

CONTENTS

FOREWORD

COME AS YOU ARE

REBECCA CAFIERO

What part of yourself have you been holding back?

Maybe it's the boldness you fear might be "too much."

Maybe it's the softness you've been told to hide.

Maybe it's the voice that says, *"this isn't who I really am."*

We're born knowing how to be fully expressed. To color outside the lines. To speak without filtering. To move through life like it's meant to be felt.

But then, life teaches us to edit.

We shrink, shape-shift, and smooth the edges to fit expectations that were never ours. We learn to trade our truth for approval. To package ourselves into polished, palatable versions of who we once were. And sometimes, we lose pieces of ourselves in the process.

That loss?

It doesn't always look dramatic. It looks like dimming your voice in a boardroom. Like staying small in a relationship. Like dressing in neutral tones when your soul craves wild color. Like not even remembering what joy felt like before responsibility weighed heavier than wonder.

Sometimes, the cost of holding back isn't just relationships, or marriages, or friendships. Sometimes, the real cost is forgetting who you are.

It cost me.

It cost me friendships. It cost me belonging. It cost me clarity. A few years after starting my entrepreneurial career, when I was first using social media to share value, my offerings and thoughts, someone I cared deeply about told me, "I just don't fit into your Instagram life."

The irony was—I wasn't performing anything. I was showing up as myself. Messy, magical, hopeful, poetic, imperfect. Some days are soft and thoughtful. Other days are fierce and on fire. But always real. And if my authenticity was threatening, it was only because it held up a mirror to someone else's disconnection.

That's the thing about being fully expressed. It will not always be met with applause. But it will always create alignment.

Because no one who is living in their own full expression is ever going to shame or silence yours.

THE PEOPLE WHO JUDGE, LIMIT, OR CENSOR
YOU ARE OFTEN THE ONES WHO HAVEN'T
GIVEN THEMSELVES PERMISSION

YET WHEN YOU SHOW UP AS THE REAL, RADIANT VERSION OF YOURSELF, YOU BECOME A MIRROR THEY'RE NOT READY TO LOOK INTO.

SO FIND OTHER MIRRORS.

The ones who reflect you back with brilliance, not distortion.

The ones who say "me too," and "go bigger," and "don't shrink now."

The ones who clap louder when you grow.

That's why this book exists.

Fully Expressed isn't just a collection of stories—it's a reclamation.

The idea for this project was sparked in a conversation with one of the women in our mastermind. She's the kind of woman who walks into a room and you feel her before you even see her. She speaks in color. Lives in texture. And her presence is a walking, talking brand experience—fiery, poetic, unforgettable, and magnetic.

As a brand designer, she doesn't just see color on the outside, she infuses it into everything she touches. Her work, her energy, even her language, is painted with passion. One day, we were talking about expression, and she said she didn't understand why people struggle to fully express themselves through their fashion. I smiled, because for her, full expression includes the art of showing up in bold colors and fun patterns.

But what struck me wasn't the vibrancy of her style. It was the truth of her expression. She wasn't dressing boldly to be seen—she was dressing in alignment with who she is.

As she beamed in turquoise and tangerine, I told her, "For you, being fully expressed looks like design, style, words, aesthetics. It's how you share your soul. For me, it's different."

I explained that as an Enneagram 7-2-8, my full expression doesn't show up in what I wear (though sequins never hurt). It shows up in how I gather women. In how I create depth and delight at the same time. In how I birth communities where truth is safe, expansion is normal, and everyone is invited to go deeper than they ever have before.

That's what full expression is to me: creating something real from your essence. Not from what's expected. But from what's true.

When I created The Pitch Club, it wasn't to give people a stage. It was to give them space. Space to show up. Space to explore. Space to be witnessed.

The first time I stood on the stage at Weekend @ the Pitch Club in Palm Springs, I nearly threw up from nerves. I questioned everything. *Who am I to be doing this?*

But a deeper voice whispered: *You dreamed this before it existed. Trust that.*

I did.

And that weekend became something I'll never forget. It wasn't perfect. But it was magic. Because I let myself be all of me. Sequins and softness. Strategy and soul. I didn't fit into a single box, and that's why it worked. Because when we allow ourselves to be all that we are, we create space for others to do the same.

I remember walking away from that event thinking: *This is what I believed life could feel like when I was little—before the world told me it couldn't.*

Before it told me that women weren't meant to collaborate like this.

Before it tried to convince me that success and soul had to live on opposite ends of the spectrum.

Before it tried to teach me that fun and depth were incompatible.

That day, I saved a photo of myself at five years old to my phone. She was radiant. Hopeful. Joyful. She believed anything was possible. And I thought: *I want to make her proud. I want to live like she dreamed I could.*

So I did.

And I still do.

This book is for her. And for every woman who has wondered if it's safe to be all of herself.

It is.

Even when it's not easy.

Because the cost of being fully expressed may be discomfort. It may be judgment. It may be losing people who were never meant to come with you.

But the cost of not being fully expressed?

That's your life. Your truth. Your joy. Your art. Your voice. Your freedom.

These twelve women said yes.

Yes to telling their truth.

Yes to stepping out of hiding.

Yes to using their voices—not the one they were taught to use—but the one they were born to use.

Each chapter in this book is a color in the spectrum of self-expression. Each voice, a note in the harmony of collective awakening. Each author, a lighthouse reminding you that you're not too much, and that you're ready to come back home to you.

Ready to shed the layers.

Ready to trust yourself.

Ready to take up space.

Ready to be.

Let this book meet you where you are. Let it stir something in you. Let it remind you that your full expression isn't just allowed, it's needed.

Because when we show up fully expressed, we don't just change ourselves.

We change every room we walk into.

We change the world.

—REBECCA CAFIERO
Founder of The Pitch Club
Publisher of *Fully Expressed*
Believer in wild women, big dreams, and bold truths

ABOUT THE AUTHOR

REBECCA CAFIERO
FOUNDER OF THE PITCH CLUB

Rebecca Cafiero is a business strategist, investor, and visibility expert helping six-, seven-, and eight-figure women entrepreneurs grow with intention and lead with impact. She's the founder of *The Pitch Club*, and a former Fortune 1000 VP of Sales with over $1B in sales experience.

Rebecca has been featured in Forbes, Women's Health, U.S. News & World Report, Daily Mail, and seen on ABC, NBC, Hulu, and American Trends Business TV. Her clients have been featured in The Wall Street Journal, NYT, Entrepreneur, People, Forbes, and Us Weekly.

Whether she's coaching a founder, speaking on stage, or appearing on-air, she blends soul and strategy to help visionary women create their next evolution—with clarity, confidence, and magic.

www.rebeccacafiero.com
Instagram: @rebeccacafiero

ONE

THE LEAKY FAUCET OF CHOOSING WHO WE ARE

AMANDA WALKER

I was sitting on a plane, thousands of feet above the earth, with *Moana 2* playing in the background while catching up on emails and creating content, when I heard this line:

"We never stop choosing who we are."

Those words landed in my chest like a truth I had always known but never fully lived.

Suddenly, I was transported back to sixth grade, standing on the playground, waiting for my two best friends to meet me, just like we did every morning. I saw them approaching, their faces unreadable. As they got closer, they handed me a folded piece of lined notebook paper. My heart leapt, anticipating something juicy about our 6th-grade crushes or recess gossip. But when I opened it, my stomach dropped.

Scrawled across the top in pencil:

The Amanda Haters Anonymous Club.

Below, a list of reasons why they had collectively decided to hate me during a sleepover I hadn't been invited to. During that sleepover, they decided they no longer wanted to be my friend.

My heart sank. Tears welled in my eyes. My whole body flushed with embarrassment and betrayal. I ran to my teacher, begging her to call my mom so I could go home and escape the humiliation.

To this day, I can still picture the exact spot on the playground where it happened. I can still see their faces, the way their expressions shifted as they watched me read that note. And I can still feel the way my heart broke.

Their reasons for hating me?

You're too bossy.
You always want to be in charge.
You act too perfect.
You're too pretty.
Blah, blah, blah.

In that moment, I internalized two life-altering beliefs:

1. Who I was . . . was wrong.
2. Don't get too close to women . . . they will break your heart.

For nearly 30 years, I guarded myself against female friendships. I lived in a version of me that was the opposite of fully expressed. I desperately wanted a best friend, but I also feared rejection for being who I truly was. I searched for proof that I was always excluded—and, unsurprisingly, I always found it.

When the spotlight turned toward me, an internal dialogue whispered that the full version of me was both *too much* and *not enough* all at the same time. It's the ache of being *too much* for some and *not enough* for others. Loud when the world wants quiet. Quiet when it demands boldness. A constant oscillation between overflow and absence—never quite fitting, always straddling the edge of "almost."

My greatest fear? Opening up my heart and sharing all the parts of me—the nooks and crannies of my soul. I had plenty of friends and colleagues, but what I craved more than anything was to be truly known.

I wish I could tell you that in my twenties or thirties I had some really cool breakthrough in my life that was a turning point to no longer question myself, that I found radical self acceptance and rode off into the sunset with a lifelong best friend.

But I don't have that story to offer.

No grand "aha" moment. No single turning point.

Instead, I spent years in a holding pattern, waiting for some comet of clarity to crash into my life and give me permission to fully accept myself. Like a plane circling the runway, waiting for permission, for clearance, for the right conditions to show me that how God made me to be was just right. It's motion, without arrival. Energy, without progress. I was going through the motions but not going anywhere. It's frustrating, exhausting, and unsustainable.

Culture tells us that transformation happens overnight—that confidence is something you turn on with a switch. But I've found it's more like a slow drip.

CONFIDENCE BUILDS IN THE QUIET MOMENTS, THE MICRO-DECISIONS, THE SMALL ACTS OF COURAGE NO ONE SEES.

The painfully sweet release of a friendship that I realized wasn't allowing me to be fully me. The vulnerability of sharing on a podcast I recorded: fully exposed vulnerability in my beliefs. Showing up to an event in an outfit that I felt so damn good in even though the look book told me I couldn't.

Like a leaky faucet of self-acceptance, steadily calling you back to the reminder that *God made you perfectly you.*

God made you with that bossiness, that quirkiness, that relentless spirit for a reason. The more you lean into it, the more free you become.

Becoming who you were truly designed to be doesn't happen in any one singular event. It's a process.

I can look back now and see that I have become new versions of myself over and over, drip by drip.

As a business owner, full expression is *everything.*

It's what builds trust with your audience. It's what creates a connection with the people you serve. It's what makes you the *purple duck in a sea of yellow ducks.*

It's not strategy or perfect branding that grows your bottom line. It's *you*—all of you.

It's one of the key elements in how I teach my community now. The world doesn't need more "coaches." It needs coaches who are all of themselves. Coaches who have passion, who have a value system, who have dragons they want to slay in their industry and aren't afraid to talk about it. The industry needs fully expressed coaches not generic, vague coaches afraid to stand out.

I know you've been there. That sinking feeling, that tightness in your chest when the world feels like it's closing in. When you feel like a fly on the wall in your own life.

But the fear of being all of you—the fear of vulnerability, of sharing your heart, your thoughts, your quirks—is far greater than the pain of staying hidden.

If the thought of sharing your deepest fears or admitting your failures makes you want to throw up—I see you. I know you.

I *am* you.

And now?

I am *all* of me.

Well, at least for now:)

Full expression isn't a finish line. It's not a one-time break-through.

It's a day-by-day, moment-by-moment journey of chipping away at anything that isn't truly you.

And the best part? The thing I once believed was my greatest weakness—the part of me that was "too much" or "too bossy"— is the very thing that makes me *so damn good* at what I do.

Holding space. Being neutral. Standing confidently in who I am.

That's my power. And you, my friend, have yours too.

Here's some powerful reflection prompts to help guide you too:

1. In what areas of your life or business do you feel the pull to be more fully expressed? What's holding you back?

2. How would your relationships, business, or life shift if you showed up as 100% yourself, unapologetically?

ABOUT THE AUTHOR

AMANDA WALKER

FOUNDER OF BEST DAMN COACH

With over 25 years of coaching experience, Amanda Walker is truly the "coach's coach." Amanda employs her background in teaching to help coaches cut through the noise, build offers that convert, and implement frameworks that transform client results and profit.

Amanda left her career as a high school teacher to build her coaching practice to multi-seven figures, and counting. She focuses on client results, helping thousands of coaches grow their confidence and coaching mastery as well as build thriving coaching practices.

Amanda Walker's passion for coaching, her unwavering commitment to her clients, and her profound impact on their lives have earned her the well-deserved reputation as the Best Damn Coach in the industry. Amanda's work has been featured in publications such as Forbes and Today Online, and on podcasts like Cubicle To CEO and more.

www.amanda-walker.com
Instagram: @awalkmyway

TWO

OBJECTS IN THE MIRROR MAY BE FARTHER THAN THEY APPEAR

EMILY JACOBSON

If you looked into a fun-house mirror and saw yourself—distorted, out of proportion—would you believe that's what you looked like? One might make your legs look five times as long as your torso; another might do the opposite. How can you reconcile conflicting images, even though both are supposed to be reflecting back the same object?

I have recently come to realize that I lived most of my life using other people as mirrors to reflect back to me who I was in order to create a picture of myself. No one asked to take on this role; not my family members, friends, teachers, or colleagues. Certainly not the acquaintances or complete strangers that I consistently used to assess my self-image. Yet, somewhere along my path, I got the memo that the image projected back to me from other people was the most reliable way to know myself.

Nothing illustrates this behavior more to me than how I chose my college major. When I got to the University of Colorado in the fall of 1996, I didn't have a clue what I wanted to study. After graduating at the top of my high school class, I enrolled in CU's School of Arts and Sciences because it seemed like the best place to explore many different disciplines. My freshman year, my favorite class was Introduction to Psychology, but I also took classes on music and biology and economics – even calculus. (I also got straight A's my first semester, which was very on-brand for me; school first, fun later.)

By the second semester of my sophomore year, I still hadn't declared a major. Perhaps sensing the need to nudge me a bit, my parents drove up to Boulder from the Denver suburbs to take me to dinner. I can still remember sitting in a booth at that restaurant across from them, trying to explain why I was having such a difficult time figuring out what I wanted to do with my life. Or, rather, I tried to explain that I was still just as lost as I was a year and a half prior.

One thing was certain in my heart, however: I wanted to do something that *mattered*. I felt deeply committed to making a difference in people's lives. As a child, I envisioned becoming a doctor when I grew up, but trying to learn the Krebs Cycle in my Intro to Biology class at CU proved to me that medicine would not be an easy path. My parents tried to shift my focus to the business school, but the Pollyanna in me wanted no part of graduating college and finding a job at some company that existed solely to make money. I'm sure my parents were stifling eye rolls as I remained steadfast in my commitment to making a difference in the world.

And then my dad said something that shifted the course of my studies, and my life: "Well, Em. It sounds like you want to work for the Feds!" The next day, I declared political science as my major.

Let me be clear. I didn't know what he was talking about. The "Feds"? Who are they? And what do they do? My dad explained to me that he was referring to the federal government. He gave examples of the countless federal agencies that served the American people, including through social programs that benefitted underprivileged communities. Now he had my attention. After connecting the dots for me between what I had learned in my high school civics class and how that translated to the real world, I left dinner feeling like he had highlighted the best option I had for pursuing a career that was about more than money or prestige. I was going to be a public servant.

My following semesters were heavy with political science classes, first the introductory ones and then the higher level ones. I got amazing grades but the truth was, I couldn't have cared less about what I was learning. Comparative politics? Snooze fest. The U.S. Presidency? I had to drag myself to class. I even got a couple of Cs my final semester, and it was not just due to having a mild case of senioritis. I was wholly uninspired by my studies.

For many years, people would ask me questions about politics, assuming that I would have strong opinions about fiscal policy or public-private partnerships or the upcoming election cycle. They would have been wrong. I was able to hide my utter disinterest in my chosen field of study by doubling down on my identity as a public servant, which was actually quite aligned with the inner knowing I had that I was destined to help people.

I managed to find a public-sector job right out of college working for the Colorado state legislature, editing bills and amendments in the nonpartisan bill drafting office. The requirement that I do my job in an unbiased manner worked well for me; it allowed me to pretend I was keeping my political opinions to myself when, in actuality, I had very few political opinions whatsoever.

I continued to manage my misaligned career path through a master's degree in public administration where I could hide behind my dedication to making government work better. I carried this public service persona with me all the way through my last government job, when I worked as a report editor in the internal audit office of the City and County of Denver. I even parlayed that into a training and consulting business where I traveled the country, teaching other government auditors how to better communicate their audit findings.

Thankfully, despite my disinterest in government (and distaste for partisan politics), I loved my work. Finding jobs that leveraged my strengths in writing and communication provided great satisfaction. And for the more than 20 years I spent grinding away with my meager pay, I found my greatest fulfillment in the relationships I cultivated with my colleagues. I was often the person in the office who people sought out when they needed someone to talk to. And believe me – I would eagerly drop whatever I was doing to lend an ear, offer advice, and respond with empathy. Whether the topic at hand was water-cooler worthy or more personal in nature, holding space for others was what truly lit me up.

It took me years to recognize that, when I was 19, I used my dad as a mirror to ask the questions, "Who am I?" and "What do I want to do with my life?" He listened to me and reflected back the best image he could construct, based on what I was saying and who he knew me to be as his daughter. He offered the image of a humble public servant, and I went on to do everything I could to make that happen.

But, what I wonder all these years later is this: Why didn't I take a look at myself and ask whether majoring in political science actually felt like a fit? Why didn't I question whether it was a good idea to go all in on something I basically knew nothing about? Maybe an even more important question is: How did I become a 19-year-old who looked for answers to such significant life decisions outside of myself?

When I look back and reflect on what I was like during my formative years, it's not terribly surprising that I grew into a young adult who couldn't even choose her own college major. My parents have told me that I was a remarkably easy child to raise. Eager to please, I followed all the rules, both at home and at school. Case-in-point, which seems ridiculous to me now: During my senior year in high school, my honors trigonometry teacher offered extra credit to anyone who came to her class on senior ditch day. That was an easy yes for me . . . not that I had any plans of participating in senior ditch day.

I relished being a good girl—a good daughter, a good student, and a good friend. My mom has shared stories of me often playing the role of mediator in my elementary school friend group, acting as the go-between when feathers were ruffled. I would get sick to my stomach at the thought of my friends being mad at each other. (Although, that discomfort was nothing compared to the full-body anxiety I would experience if anyone was mad at *me*.)

All this rule following and goodness paired well with my ultimate badge of honor: people pleaser. I was selfless and giving, constantly sizing up the needs of other people and twisting myself into pretzels to find ways to help them. I even won an award at summer camp one year that recognized campers who put others' needs before their own. The ultimate chameleon, I could mold myself to fit into pretty much any situation. And I had very few opinions. "Go along to get along" was a way of life for me and a reliable source for being accepted by others.

Perhaps all of this helping energy I was exuding and peace keeping I was doing was benign. Doesn't the world need more people who are willing to sacrifice for the greater good? During those formative years, I wasn't thinking about whether my intentions were pure. But as I look back, I can see the deeper purpose behind my behavior. With every good deed, every action praised, I was looking for some sort of positive reaction or assessment of value.

Through my actions, I was constantly gathering information from others to compile an understanding about who I was as a human being. Every person who was a recipient of my agreeable and generous nature served as a mirror for me. If a teacher told me I was a good student, then that meant I was a good student, and more importantly a good person. When my mom thanked me for being so helpful at home, I took that to mean I was valuable. When a boss lavished praise on me for being indispensable, I could rest easy knowing that I mattered.

This strategy of using nearly every person you interact with as a mirror works well enough until someone reflects back something negative. It also back-fires when you actually need something.

Ultimately, for years I was sacrificing authenticity for acceptance. Thankfully, I found my way into therapy at age 43 to address the discomfort that was building internally, the source of which I couldn't quite put my finger on. I can see clearly now that it was the decades of suppressing my true needs, desires, and opinions that had taken a toll on me; all I knew at the time was that very little in my life felt right.

I'll forever be grateful that I somehow found my way to the gifted therapist who I drove 45 minutes to see weekly for nearly a year. She was in Boulder—my college town—and I relished not only the transformative sessions I had with her, but the reflective time I had in the car on the way home. I had always had a positive association with therapy; I never saw it as a weakness but rather a supportive intervention when life gets tough.

Although I had dabbled in therapy here and there to cope with challenging issues and seasons, I had never worked with anyone as dynamic as this particular practitioner. She introduced me to concepts like attachment styles, polyvagal theory, and Internal Family Systems. She helped me understand the importance of your therapist being trauma informed, and I gained a much broader understanding of what trauma actually is. And, through her expert use of somatic interventions, I was finally able to connect with my body in a way I never had before.

I had always considered myself to be in touch with my emotions, but I wasn't aware of how cerebral I was about my relationship with them. During one particularly angry session, I remember her asking me where I felt my anger. This inquiry made zero sense to me. "What do you mean, where do I feel angry? I don't feel it. I just *am*."

It was almost as if my emotions lived in my mind but stopped at my neck. My therapist challenged me to scan my body and locate where the sensation of anger was showing up. It took a lot of practice, but I finally recognized that anger always showed up at the base of my skull. That began the process of reacquainting myself with truly living—and experiencing emotions—in my body.

Facing my deepest fear in therapy was what allowed me to finally recognize the profound limitations of my misguided attempts at self-understanding. I didn't even know what my deepest fear was until I stumbled upon it during one of my sessions: If no one reflects back to me who I am, I cease to exist. I had been working through some anxieties about being judged by others for (finally) making a change in my career path. My mind was tangled up in worries about leaving behind a 20-year career in public service to become a life coach. What would people think?

I had become nearly paralyzed with fear imagining the reactions I might get from colleagues, acquaintances, and family members: "How weird." "What is going on with her?" "What is she doing?" "Did she have a mid-life crisis?" Imagining the absence of the reflections I had worked so hard to consistently receive for decades—helpful, kind, good, and worthy—I imagined that anything else would reflect the opposite. At worst, in the absence of being seen as helpful, kind, good, and worthy, I would be perceived as nothing at all. After all, who was I if these things were stripped from me? Talk about an existential crisis.

Worse even than looking into a fun-house mirror, this experience was like looking into a mirror that was shattered. And that's exactly what it took to see the dark side of a lifetime of outsourcing my sense-of-self to others. Each of my seemingly innocent behaviors, when I took a closer look at them, reflected so many unhealthy patterns:

- Codependent thinking and people pleasing
- Hiding my true thoughts and desires
- Dismissing my needs as unimportant
- Self-sacrificing followed by angry outbursts when I reach a limit I never communicated
- Hiding my truth to avoid judgment
- Trying to fix other people's problems, acting as their savior
- Not tuning into my body's emotional experience
- Taking on other people's emotions as my own

Even though seeing my tendencies in a new light was painful, it was also liberating. Understanding why I was doing what I was doing, and to have compassion for myself in the process, opened up new ways of being. For the first time, I endeavored to go inward and ask who I truly was, looking in my own internal mirror.

During this process, I was able to see that I am indeed helpful, kind, good, and worthy, but not because other people say I am. Rather, I could see these traits in myself. I also discovered that I'm so many other things that no one had been reflecting back to me. I realized that I am opinionated. I am not like everyone else around me. I am quirky and neuro-spicy and endlessly fascinated by the human condition. I love psychology, and even though I didn't follow the spark that ignited in my college psychology class, I realized it wasn't too late to course-correct.

After experiencing these therapy-induced revelations, I considered going back to school to get another master's degree, this time in psychology. However, the newly discovered rule-breaker in me decided that I could achieve similar outcomes through coaching. And, I'd make my own mark on the coaching world by incorporating nervous system regulation as a differentiator in what I offered my clients.

Shortly after my year-long therapy journey, I had discovered the power of a modality called Neuro-Somatic Intelligence, which helped me feel safe enough to embody my new inner knowing. Once I experienced the power of leveraging the nervous system to facilitate transformation, I knew I couldn't keep it to myself; I had to share it with anyone who was experiencing the same struggles with perfectionism, authenticity, and people-pleasing.

After completely changing the trajectory of my career—a course correct, perhaps?—I think it's possible that I am still a public servant. My public service may no longer be delivered through proofreading legislation or editing audit reports, but through the one-on-one connection that I always savored. In my new career, I'm helping members of the public feel safe enough in their own inner knowing that they can go out and serve the public in their own way. And that's a reflection of my true self that I can finally feel very, very good about.

IF YOU'VE EVER LOOKED IN THE MIRROR AND WONDERED WHO WAS STARING BACK—IF THE VERSION OF YOURSELF THAT OTHERS SEE HAS EVER FELT MISALIGNED WITH THE TRUTH INSIDE YOU—TAKE THAT AS A SIGN. NOT OF SOMETHING WRONG, BUT OF SOMETHING READY TO BE RECLAIMED.

Start small. Start inside. Ask: *What am I feeling right now—and where do I feel it in my body?* Not to judge it. Not to fix it. Just to notice.

That noticing? It's how we begin to return to ourselves. It's how we trade performance for presence, shape-shifting for sovereignty.

This is nervous system work. This is identity work. And it's possible—for all of us.

Curious to learn more about guiding your nervous system to better somatic responses? Check out my Nervous System Cheat Sheet here:

https://emily-jacobson-coaching.kit.com/somatic-yes-no

ABOUT THE AUTHOR

EMILY JACOBSON

SOMATIC LIFE COACH AND STATE SHIFTER FOR PURPOSE-DRIVEN WOMEN

Emily Jacobson is a Somatic Coach and creator of the State Shift Session—a 30-minute nervous system reset designed to help people feel calmer, clearer, and more in control in real life. Through one-on-one sessions, group programs, and corporate workshops, Emily teaches practical, science-backed tools to shift your state and expand your capacity to grow, lead, and live fully expressed.

With a background in public service, communications, and transformational coaching, she brings both structure and soul to her work—making complex nervous system concepts feel simple, personal, and actionable. Whether she's guiding a high-achiever through burnout or helping a parent find peace in the chaos, Emily's work is rooted in one simple truth: when your body feels safe, everything changes.

www.emilyjacobson.com
Instagram: @emilyjacobsoncoaching

THREE

SCRATCHING THE ITCH

CARRIE MURRAY

"COME ON, GIRLS
DO YOU BELIEVE IN LOVE?
'CAUSE I GOT SOMETHING TO SAY ABOUT IT
AND IT GOES SOMETHING LIKE THIS"
- MADONNA

Madonna really *did* have it right with this one—this song is basically a glitter-covered megaphone shouting, *"Girl, know your worth!"* It's a rallying cry for women to value themselves and hold out for relationships built on emotional honesty, real connection, and none of that "bare minimum" nonsense.

Now, choosing to live like a queen every day, not always easy. Sometimes it means saying "no thanks" to charming-but-emotionally-unavailable people, or walking away from relationships that sparkle on the outside but are hollow on the inside (kinda like a chocolate Easter bunny). But doing so reminds the world—and yourself—that you deserve to be uplifted, cherished, and respected in every area of life: physically, personally, and yes, professionally too.

AND IF YOU REMEMBER NOTHING ELSE FROM THIS CHAPTER, LET ME BE THE LITTLE VOICE IN YOUR HEAD (WITH A CROWN AND A SASSY WINK) SAYING: *YOU ARE A QUEEN.* ACT ACCORDINGLY.

That means no discounting yourself, no playing small, and absolutely no settling for someone who can't handle your shine.

Be bold, be expressive, and if they're not ready for all that magic—kindly show them the exit.

It's so easy to write these words. It's easy to say them. It's even easier to slap them onto an Instagram caption with a cute filter and call it a day. And honestly? It's easy to read them in the comfort of this book, nod along, then quietly close it and never think about them again.

But I'm here to tell you: *don't close the book just yet.*

Because actually living a fully expressed life? That's *daily* work. And not "daily work" like walking your dog while sipping coffee and listening to a podcast. I mean the kind of work that requires presence, courage, and consistency—especially when life gets sticky or knocks you slightly off balance.

Staying in the zone of full expression isn't something you check off a list. It's ongoing. It's uncomfortable. It's exactly like that moment in yoga when you're twisting, sweating, and suddenly your boobs are so squished together you're thinking, *is everyone staring at my cleavage right now?* (They should, it's poppin') And then the instructor whispers, "Breathe . . . stay with it."

And you're like, *Excuse me? Breathe? In this torture pose?*

I mean . . . *Chair pose?* Why is it so hard?!

My thighs are shaking, my soul is leaving my body, and you want me to *relax?*

Exactly. That's what full expression feels like sometimes. Ridiculous, raw, a little sweaty, and entirely worth it—if you stay with it.

And funny enough, we're actually *wired* for it. According to Jean Piaget, *The Origins of Intelligence in Children* (1952), between 18 months and three years old, toddlers are just beginning to understand that they exist as individuals—separate from others. This is when they start asserting independence, testing limits, saying *"no!"* and *"mine!"* with bold conviction. It's not defiance—it's development. It's the beginning of self-expression and if you witnessed it, it's so damn cute and humbling at the same time. They are living FULLY EXPRESSED. No fear of judgement! That's why we see them in a grocery store dressed as Elsa with a Spiderman mask. NO FEAR of being themselves.

So if toddlers can claim their space in the world with messy, unapologetic energy—maybe we can take a page from their (sticky, toy tossing) book. Maybe full expression isn't about perfection. Maybe it's about allowing yourself to show up—boldly, clumsily, imperfectly—and still say, *"This is me."*

So that fully expressive version of yourself has been in hibernation for some time and it's time to wake them because we have some things to get done!

My mom was one of the only moms I knew who worked. She started as a secretary, eventually moved up the ranks, and even went to college as an adult. We actually took a math class together because we were in college at the same time.

My journey to full expression was not direct, linear, or clear cut. But it began when I chose a new path forward at 18. I was the first person in my family to graduate from college. As the first, we never really talked about college as a family. My parents assumed I would go straight to work, so when I told them I wanted to pursue higher education, they were both shocked and excited to see me chase my dreams.

I initially pursued a career in social work, focusing on domestic violence prevention. But after two years working as a court advocate in the San Francisco DA's office, I found the work emotionally draining and realized I needed to make a change.

What followed was a series of career pivots—from aspiring actor to public school teacher and principal. It was in the role of principal that I felt the most confined, restricted, and furthest from my true self. I loved being a teacher. The innovation, creativity, and routine were things I thrived in, and I never really found it "too hard." I loved creating a micro-community of learners and designing lesson plans to meet the diverse needs of my students. I mean, how many different ways can you teach fractions? Hundreds! I used them all to meet the needs of every learner in my classroom.

I thrived in that environment, but I began to feel restless, that familiar itch I'd come to recognize as a sign that something deeper was calling me. So, I pursued my administrative credential and became a principal. But within less than two years, I realized this role didn't just fail to scratch the itch, it magnified it. It was one of the hardest things I've ever done, and I constantly felt like I was failing. For the first time, I felt uncertain and couldn't even look my teachers, families, and students in the eye. I had to make extremely difficult decisions that impacted all of them—everything from hiring and firing, to meetings with parents desperate for support for their child with special needs. I would promise to do our best, all while knowing we didn't have the budget, manpower, or resources. It was ROUGH.

Enrollment was at an all-time low. Public schools are funded by Average Daily Attendance (ADA), and the disparity between what the state provides and what's needed to operate is vast. Grants and fundraising are essential to a school's survival. I felt like I was phoning it in, even while receiving praise from teachers, the executive director, and families. They told me I was doing a great job, but internally, I thought, "I could be doing so much more."

I kept asking myself: Why don't I love what I'm good at? Shouldn't I love something I'm being praised and recognized for? But it just didn't feel like me. The idea of spending the rest of my career making decisions that could profoundly have a detrimental impact on families and children was unbearable.

There was also a small group of students who were being quietly passed around from teacher to teacher because we didn't have the resources to support them. These students were known as "Twice Exceptional"— both intellectually gifted and learning-different. Most of them were between the ages of five and eight. Our campus had three of them. So not enough to fill a classroom and different in age so they couldn't be in the same grade level either.

So, I made the leap and opened my own private school. How hard could it be? That leap into entrepreneurship changed everything. For the first time, I felt true autonomy. No one was above me telling me how to do things. I could finally trust that all my experience and education would pay off.

I had the knowledge, the financial support, the cutest little campus with a playground, two great teachers, eight families, and two support staff. We launched our kindergarten classroom with the goal of adding a new grade each year. We built a curriculum tailored to each child, letting them reach milestones at their own pace. I had never felt more like myself: as a leader, educator, advocate. I was working hard, and it felt amazing.

Our first year was a huge success—except for one major issue: I knew how to teach and run a school, but I didn't know how to run a business. From the outside, we looked like we were crushing it. But on paper, we were running out of funding—fast. I had to seek support.

Networking events were my first stop. Most were filled with older white men who barely acknowledged me. I kept thinking, "Where are all the women? Where are the women business owners?" This was before anyone said the phrase "Girl Boss."

Eventually, I had to make the hard decision to close the school. The students transitioned to another school on our shared campus. My teachers were quickly hired by others because of their specialized experience. But I was left wondering: if I had found the right support system—mentors, advisors, peers—could I have built a stronger foundation?

That itch came back.

I started to think about how women like Sara Blakely, Kate Spade, and Oprah did it. They had something in common: they were surrounded by like-minded people who challenged and supported them. They were resilient, resourceful . . . and not alone.

Frustrated, I hosted my own networking event/dinner party. Six women entrepreneurs showed up and were so grateful to have a space that didn't feel spammy or salesy or sterile. That first dinner was a success. Soon, I was hosting dinner parties in my backyard—an accountant, a photographer, an event designer, a hairstylist. Casual conversations over home-cooked meals turned into powerful collaborations. We didn't see each other as competition. We set strategic pricing, shared advice, and supported one another.

Before I knew it, 20 women were gathered in my backyard on a fall evening. I realized it was time for a website and directory. A space to showcase these women, offer mentorship for new entrepreneurs, and programming to help established ones thrive. I knew I wanted it to reflect an unapologetically feminine approach to entrepreneurship.

And that's how the Business Relationship Alliance—BRA Network—was born in 2015.

For the first time since leaving the classroom, I felt like myself again. I wasn't itchy. I was fully alive in my role. BRA became one of the largest networking groups for women entrepreneurs in Los Angeles with over 300 members. The pandemic didn't slow us down. We were already 75% online and had a strong digital presence. Our community grew beyond LA and became global.

Over the last nine years:

- We partnered with nonprofits to raise funds.
- We created educational courses I wish I had access to when I opened my school.
- We hosted a conference all about money, finance, investing, and funding—on a yacht, no less!
- We created awards to honor visionary and empowering women.
- We launched a podcast to share our members' stories, yet another resource I wish I'd had while navigating my first dive into entrepreneurship.

I learned how to show up as my full, authentic self. It became easy because I was aligned with my purpose. I knew who I was serving, how I could help, and the value I brought. My best self was being fully expressed—and it felt effortless.

Today, BRA Network is a thriving online platform where women entrepreneurs connect, get hired, and support each other. We've facilitated over 1,000 collaborations, generated hundreds of thousands in revenue, and secured over $2 million in funding for members.

I'm incredibly proud of what I've built and the hundreds of women I've helped realize their dreams—some they never even thought possible.

In the winter of 2024, I settled into my usual BRA morning... and felt that familiar itch again. But this time, I welcomed it. It's my signal that something new and exciting is coming.

I found myself reflecting on the hundreds of women I've helped achieve their dreams—and how I had given them the blueprint to make them happen. While I felt deeply fulfilled professionally, I began to recognize that the new itch I was feeling was my own dreams calling out to be fulfilled. I came to understand that supporting other women in reaching their dreams was exactly what I needed in order to begin pursuing my own.

That inner itch wasn't just restlessness—it was the purpose. It was my own voice asking for a platform, my own story demanding to be told. And now, I'm answering that call with *Carrie On!*, my new web series and podcast. It's more than content, it's a movement. *Carrie On!* is a safe space for women to engage in socially and emotionally conscious conversations while sharing their talents and truths. It's a platform where our stories matter, where our voices are lifted, and where our presence is undeniable. We will not be muted, dismissed, or ignored. This is our moment to speak, to connect, and to carry on, together.

CARRIE MURRAY

FOUNDER OF THE BRA NETWORK AND THE WEALTHY WOMEN'S SUMMIT

Carrie Murray is the founder of the BRA Network and a catalyst for marginalized coaches, creatives, and consultants. Through strategic connections and collaborations, Carrie is a superconnector leading the movement for greater support, storytelling, and connection within the fabric of entrepreneurship.

Her new project, *Carrie On!,* will spotlight the moving stories of marginalized artists, creatives, and trailblazers of all walks of life. In a time when American society is turning a blind eye on diversity and differences, Carrie is putting a spotlight on it.

www.bra-network.com/
Instagram: @_carriemurray_ & @bra_network_

FOUR

UNAPOLOGETICALLY BRANDED

SARA CHAMBERS

A fully expressed woman is dangerous to those who benefit from the power structures she dares to challenge.

To be fully expressed is an act of integrity, honesty, and a commitment to unfastening the anchors intended to keep us small, buried, quiet, and complacent. A fully expressed woman isn't tethered to the expectations of others, and she's harder to control, manipulate, and break.

The transformational impact of knowing, owning, and expressing your full self is also a radical act of service. Your authentic expression in business, in personal identity, in creative ventures, and in how you move through the world signals to others that they too can have permission to challenge the limited representations they see presented to them.

When we stay hidden in the silence of the monotony—the sameness, the uniformity of everyone around us—we blend in and perpetuate the very status quo that we're all working so hard to dismantle.

Hiding feels safe.

When no one notices us, we can slide into the background unseen. We can dissolve into the crowd, and no one will challenge us, ask more of us, or criticize us.

But it all comes at a cost that is far too expensive.

It's costing you aligned opportunities that are perfectly formed for your unique blend of skills, experience, passions, and talents.

The kinds of opportunities that create joy and purpose in your lived experience.

It's costing you relationships built on trust, intimacy, and connection.

The kinds of relationships that celebrate you, challenge you, and allow you to move through the world in love. We aren't created to be in isolation, and when you're not showing up in the truth of who you are, you're inviting in others who are misaligned. You'll end up in a room full of people while also feeling more alone than ever.

It's costing you your integrity of self.

You're the only one who will be with you in every moment. You're the only one who will witness every heartbreak, champion every accomplishment, feel every loss, and relish in every obstacle overcome. No matter who comes in and out of your life, you're the only one there in each season; you can't escape yourself.

But abandoning yourself in service of quiet waters only creates a storm within.

It's time for you to stand in the light and be seen not as a watered-down, palatable, conformed version of yourself, but rather as a woman who lives in her truth with the courage to allow others to see.

EXPRESSION IS COMMUNICATION —THE POWER OF BEING SEEN

Communication is the pathway of connection from one soul to another, and embodied, authentic expression of self is the only way we have to show others who we are and invite the kind of relationships, opportunities, and life we're calling in.

But when we think about communication, we often reduce it to just words: what we say, how we say it, and the way in which others respond.

> IN REALITY, COMMUNICATION IS SO MUCH MORE THAN JUST SPOKEN LANGUAGE. IT'S THE WAY WE MOVE, THE WAY WE PRESENT OURSELVES, THE CHOICES WE MAKE, THE SPACES WE OCCUPY, AND THE ENERGY WE BRING INTO A ROOM.

We are constantly signaling to others, whether we realize it or not. Every choice we make—consciously or unconsciously—is a form of communication:

- **Body language:** The way we hold ourselves, whether we shrink or stand tall, make eye contact or look away. Confidence, discomfort, openness, and resistance are all communicated before a single word is spoken.

- **Personal style:** The clothes we wear, the colors we choose, the way we adorn ourselves. All of these send messages about who we are, what we value, and how we want to be perceived.
- **Creative expression:** Art, music, writing, dance. These are all languages of their own, each telling a story that words sometimes cannot.
- **Digital presence:** The way we engage online, the content we share, the way we present our businesses or brands. These are all curated forms of communication that influence how others see us.
- **Silence:** Even in the absence of words, we are still speaking. The decision *not* to voice an opinion, *not* to take up space, *not* to show up fully. These too are signals, often of fear, restraint, or a learned habit of staying small.

At its core, expression is communication, and communication is how we form relationships, build trust, and create meaning in our lives. If we suppress our expression, we limit our ability to truly connect. When we stay hidden, we aren't just hiding from visibility—we're hiding from the relationships, opportunities, and experiences that would allow us to thrive.

To be fully seen requires full honesty. Yet, for so many of us, honesty feels like a risk, one we've been conditioned to avoid.

For generations, conformity has been a survival strategy for women.

Hiding, not rocking the boat, and being agreeable weren't just about social acceptance; they were about safety. Staying quiet, small, and digestible was how women avoided conflict, punishment, exile, and even danger.

History has shown us the cost of stepping out of line. The women's suffrage movement, the fight for reproductive rights, the demand for workplace equality, all of these were met with resistance, sometimes violent. Women who were outspoken were shamed, ostracized, or silenced. We were taught—explicitly and implicitly—that our power was a threat to the structures that kept men in control. And so, we learned to minimize ourselves to survive.

- We stayed silent when we had something to say.
- We smoothed our edges to avoid making others uncomfortable.
- We prioritized acceptance over authenticity.
- We became palatable, digestible, easy to consume.

Because that's what kept us safe. That's what was expected.

But safety and freedom are not the same thing.

We live in a time when women have more agency, more visibility, and more opportunities than ever before. The world is no longer as rigidly stacked against us, but the echoes of those old survival mechanisms still live in our bones. Many of us are still shrinking, still playing small, still prioritizing likability over truth—even when we don't have to.

That's not to say the risks of full expression have disappeared. Even today, women who step fully into their voice, their power, and their identity still face criticism, judgment, and backlash. The difference is that we now have a choice. We are no longer bound by the same rules of silence. We don't have to keep making ourselves small to be safe.

I've learned that the hard way when my expression cost me dearly.

For a long time, I believed that my role as a senior copywriter at a global humanitarian organization was not just a job—it was deeply tied to my purpose, my values, and my identity. I wanted to do work that mattered, to contribute to something bigger than myself. I poured my skills, energy, and strategic thinking into the organization, believing that being excellent at my job was enough.

But it wasn't.

I quickly learned that being good at your work isn't always the thing that makes you valuable in a system that prioritizes conformity over innovation. I was exceptional at what I did, but I also asked hard questions. I challenged inefficiencies. I spoke up when things weren't being done well. I expected people to take their responsibilities seriously, not just for their own sake but for the mission we were serving. And for that, I was labeled *difficult*.

I was told I was *too much*.

Too opinionated.

Too outspoken.

Too unwilling to let things slide.

I carried that weight for a long time, wondering if I needed to soften myself, to be less, to take up less space in order to belong.

One year on Halloween, I walked into my office dressed as Cruella de Vil, fully expecting to win the office costume contest, and I walked out without a job.

I was told my position had been eliminated. But the message was clear: I was no longer a *good culture fit*.

That day could have felt like a failure. It could have sent me spiraling into self-doubt, believing that I was the problem, that I needed to shrink myself in order to succeed.

Instead, it was the greatest redirection of my life.

That was the last day I would ever sit across from someone and try to convince them I was the best person for the job. That was the moment I decided to never again put myself in an environment that required me to be smaller.

So, I took my three-month severance and started my own business.

At first, it was survival. A mixture of hurt, spite, and blind ambition. I didn't have a perfect plan—just a fire in my chest and a refusal to ever again sit across from someone who couldn't see my value.

I gathered up everything I had learned in my years working across marketing, copywriting, design, and public relations, and I began offering my services to anyone who needed them. I wrote websites, crafted brand messaging, built pitch decks, created social content, designed logos, and helped people tell their stories, anything that allowed me to use my skills to make something meaningful.

What started as a scrappy hustle slowly began to take shape. I realized that everything I loved—the words, the visuals, the strategy—was ultimately about communication. Expression. Identity. And more than anything, I was drawn to helping women build businesses that looked and felt like *them*.

Over time, my work sharpened into creative storytelling, strategic branding, and championing women as they stepped more fully into their businesses and themselves. I found purpose in helping women show up honestly and powerfully, using their brand as the vehicle to reflect who they are and what they stand for.

That business—born from heartbreak and fueled by defiance—has since grown into something deeply meaningful and increasingly successful year over year. It is no longer about proving myself to the world that underestimated me. It's about liberation through self-expression. It's about making space for women to be fully seen, fully heard, and fully respected—not just in how they do business, but in how they exist.

And in the seven years since, I've realized something powerful:

The very qualities that made me "wrong" in a rigid work environment are the exact qualities that make me an exceptional entrepreneur.

The sharp thinking, the unwillingness to accept mediocrity, the ability to see things from a higher perspective and ask the tough questions—all of the things that made me difficult to contain within someone else's system—became the foundation for building my own.

That experience gave me the permission slip I had been too scared to write for myself.

And from that moment forward, I made a promise:

- I would no longer try to fit into spaces that weren't built for me.
- I would no longer shrink myself for someone else's comfort.
- I would no longer seek validation from people who were threatened by my light.

Instead, I would seek spaces, opportunities, and relationships where I could be fully expressed—where my leadership, my ideas, my voice, and my presence weren't just tolerated but embraced.

Because the truth is, I don't want to be successful in environments that force me to be a smaller version of myself.

I don't want to be in relationships where I have to tiptoe around my own personality.

I don't want to be in rooms where my presence is seen as a threat rather than an inspiration.

I want to build spaces where people are encouraged to shine—where my light inspires others to turn up their own brightness, not dim mine.

Being fully expressed is not just an act of personal freedom, it's a radical act of leadership.

So, what if, instead of contorting ourselves to fit, we allowed ourselves to be seen? What if expression—true, full, unfiltered expression—wasn't just a risk but a revolution?

What if the most radical thing we could do was take up space and in it, we found our purpose wrapped in our personal truth?

As a brand strategist, I meet people every day who still think branding is logos and colors. And while it's more than that, branding *is* in fact design. Not just design in the exclusively visual sense but in the strategic and intentional creation of something fully expressed.

Branding, at its core, is about visibility. Not just being seen but being recognized, being understood, being felt. When branding is done right, it's not about crafting an illusion—it's about revealing a truth.

It's unique. It's purposeful. It's honest.

And the same is true for personal expression.

Just like a brand, you can show up in two ways:

1. You can shape yourself into what you think people want, molding yourself to be accepted.
2. Or you can do the deep, necessary work of understanding who you are, how you're different, and what you bring—and then unapologetically embody that.

The first path is easier. It gives you the comfort of fitting in, of feeling safe in the short term. But it's also the path to exhaustion, misalignment, and an inevitable loss of self.

The second path? It's harder, but it's the one that leads to real, lasting connection. The kind that doesn't require you to perform.

The kind that invites the right people, the right opportunities, and the right experiences into your life—not because you've manipulated yourself to be *liked*, but because you've allowed yourself to be *known*.

In the branding space, my purpose is not to tell women who they are, it's to reflect back to them who they already are becoming.

The most powerful work I do is helping women see themselves clearly, maybe for the first time. Because when you see yourself—when you recognize your own power, your own uniqueness, your own value—you become unstoppable.

THE JOURNEY TO FULL EXPRESSION

For many of us, full expression is not our default—it's a journey. We aren't born afraid to be seen, to take up space, or to speak our truth. That fear is learned and reinforced by a world that rewards palatability over authenticity. We are shaped by environments that teach us which parts of ourselves are acceptable and which need to be softened, silenced, or erased. I know this because I lived it—told I was "too much" for asking hard questions, pushing for excellence, and refusing to play small. That experience didn't just mark the end of a job—it revealed just how often we're asked to trade our full expression for approval.

And so we learn to make ourselves smaller before anyone even asks us to.

We don't hold back for no reason. We do it because we've learned where it's *not safe* to be fully ourselves.

- **Workplaces that demand conformity.** Many professional environments reward compliance over innovation, likability over leadership, and teamwork over truth. The people who challenge systems, push for excellence, or refuse to settle for mediocrity often find themselves labeled as *difficult* rather than *visionary*.
- **Relationships that expect palatability.** Sometimes, the people closest to us are the ones most invested in us staying the same. Our friendships, families, and partnerships can carry unspoken rules about how much we're allowed to change, how much space we can take up, and what's considered *acceptable* expression.
- **Social settings that demand sameness.** The world tells us to blend in—to be likable, easygoing, digestible. We see this pressure everywhere: in the way women are expected to be agreeable, to smooth over conflict, to make themselves attractive but not *too* bold, confident but not *too* assertive.

- **The internalized voice of self-censorship.** Long before anyone else can judge us, we often judge ourselves first. We silence our own ideas before they leave our lips. We water down our opinions before we even share them. We shrink to avoid the discomfort of *possibly* being rejected, when in reality, we've already rejected ourselves.

But the cost of hiding is steep. Every time we censor ourselves, we reinforce the very structures that are designed to keep us small.

One of the biggest barriers to full expression is the fear of being too much: too loud, too opinionated, too ambitious, too sensitive. Many of us learned at an early age that standing out wasn't always rewarded. Instead, we were conditioned to believe that our bigness made us burdensome, that our opinions made us difficult, that our emotions made us weak.

I know this fear intimately.

When I lost my job, it wasn't because I wasn't good at my work. It was because I was *too good* at seeing inefficiencies, *too willing* to ask questions, *too unwilling* to settle for doing things the way they'd always been done.

And for a moment, I wondered if they were right. I wondered if I *was* too much.

But over time, I realized that my ability to challenge, to innovate, to see what others ignored—those were strengths, not liabilities. I wasn't too much; I was simply too big for a space that was too small for me.

And that's when I understood something critical:

Being fully expressed isn't just about owning your voice, it's also about choosing to be in the right rooms.

So, what does full expression feel like?

For so long, I thought full expression would feel like too much. But in reality, it feels like alignment.

- It feels like **relief**—the deep exhale of no longer contorting yourself to be something you're not.
- It feels like **ease**—the energy you reclaim when you stop filtering your every thought, word, and action.
- It feels like **power**—the magnetism that comes from showing up so fully that you begin attracting the people, opportunities, and experiences that were always meant for you.

And the most surprising part?

When we are fully expressed, we give others permission to do the same.

Every time I've stepped more fully into my own voice, I've seen it reflected back to me in the women I work with. They feel the shift. They see the way I own my truth, and it creates a ripple effect—a realization that *they, too, can stop shrinking*.

But if we want to do this, really be fully expressed, we have to also detach from both criticism and praise.

Here's what I mean.

The fear of judgment is often the biggest barrier to full expression. But here's the thing: both negative and positive feedback can be traps.

- If you let *criticism* shape you, you'll constantly shrink and adjust to avoid discomfort.
- If you let *praise* define you, you'll find yourself performing for approval rather than standing firm in your truth.

At some point, you have to ask yourself: If no one praised me, and no one criticized me, who would I be?

Because full expression isn't about validation. It's about freedom. But that freedom is going to trigger a lot of people.

One of the most uncomfortable realities of full expression is this: When you fully express yourself, you become a mirror.

Some people will see you stepping into your power and feel *inspired*. They'll see a new possibility for themselves. They'll be drawn to you because your authenticity gives them permission to embrace their own.

But others will see you and feel *threatened*. Your boldness will remind them of all the ways they've kept themselves small. Your courage will highlight their fear. And instead of rising to meet their own potential, they'll try to pull you back down.

Not because you're wrong.

Not because you're too much.

But because they aren't ready to see what's possible for them.

And that's okay.

The truth is, not everyone will love your full expression. But the right people—the ones who see you, who celebrate you, who are inspired by you—*will find you.*

And that's worth everything.

The world does not need more people who know how to shrink. It does not need more women who have mastered the art of staying small, staying agreeable, staying safe inside the expectations of others.

The world needs you, fully expressed.

- Not the version of you that is palatable.
- Not the version of you that is easier to digest.
- Not the version of you that is shaped by fear of judgment.

The *real* you. The one who has something to say, something to create, something to contribute. The one who has always known, deep down, that she was meant to take up space.

Because when you step into full expression, you don't just change your own life—you create permission for others to do the same. You become the lighthouse, standing boldly in your truth, illuminating the path for those still afraid to take the first step.

And make no mistake: this is not an easy journey. There will be resistance. From others, from systems, from the small voice inside you that still wonders if it's safer to hide. But the cost of staying quiet, of staying small, of staying unseen is far greater than the cost of stepping into the light.

So here is my invitation to you:

What is one small way you can step into fuller expression today?

Maybe it's using your voice in a conversation where you'd normally stay quiet.

Maybe it's sharing something unfiltered—without over-editing yourself.

Maybe it's wearing something bold, writing something honest, making a choice that aligns with *who you really are*, not who you think you need to be.

Whatever it is, take the step.

Because the more you express, the more you become.

And if you're ready to go deeper—to uncover your full expression in your brand, your work, and your leadership—I'd love to walk this path with you. My work is about helping women like you show up fully, boldly, and unapologetically.

If you're ready to claim your space, let's do it together. Visit our website to begin your transformation now.

ABOUT THE AUTHOR

SARA CHAMBERS

CEO, CREATIVE DIRECTOR, AND BRAND STRATEGIST AT ELLY AND NORA CREATIVE

Sara Chambers is a brand strategist and the CEO of Elly and Nora Creative, a full-service agency that builds brave, bold, brag-worthy brands for entrepreneurs who are ready to lead with purpose and power. With a background in marketing, PR, and communications for nonprofits and a variety of lifestyle brands, Sara has spent nearly two decades helping thought leaders clarify their message, amplify their mission, and own their space. She's also the founder of Chicks Who Give a Hoot, a nonprofit mobilizing women entrepreneurs as a force for good through media, mentorship, and community.

www.ellyandnoracreative.com
Instagram:
@sarachamberscreative
@ellyandnoracreative
@chickswhogiveahoot

FIVE

UNMASKING THE CHAMELEON: LEARNING AUTHENTIC EXPRESSION

MORGAN MILLS

The room was filled with chatter that felt like white noise, the clink-ing of glasses a stark contrast to the sudden silence in my head. I scanned the sea of faces at the networking event—not a single one mirrored mine. A familiar unease settled in, a cold prickle at the back of my neck. *Don't be too loud. Don't be too aggressive. Don't be too much.*

The whispers of American society about Black culture, the ones that had been drilled into me since childhood, echoed in my mind. I took a breath, and the chameleon took over. My voice soft-ened, my posture straightened, I got a little more perky, my dialect shifted, and the words I'd naturally use vanished. I was performing, not existing. Another mental reset, another layer of myself tucked away.

It's a dance many high-achieving minority women know well: the constant code-switching, the silent negotiation of identity. You morph to fit, not because you're weak but because you're strategic. You want to connect, to be seen, to avoid the tired, harmful stereotypes. But the truth is, this constant adaptation, this careful curation of self, is exhausting. And it's a mask. A mask that, when worn too long, imprints on your skin, blurring the lines of who you truly are.

To be fully expressed is to shed that mask. It's to embrace every facet of yourself, to honor your authentic voice, and in doing so, to honor the world around you. It's about showing up as your complete self, especially in spaces that weren't always built for you. For women in business, this is crucial. The constant 'doing' and the pressure to fit labels can lead you astray, leaving you lost in a maze of expectations.

But this journey isn't a smooth one. There will be moments when the mask feels like your only shield, when slipping into the chameleon's skin seems like the safest choice. Yet, that very strength—the ability to adapt—becomes a weakness when it leads to self-erasure. You begin to feel like a stranger in your own life, questioning your identity, losing sight of your core. So, I invite you to join me as I navigate the path of reclaiming my voice, embracing my whole self, and showing up authentically—for myself, for my loved ones, for my clients, and for the world.

It's not a single memory but a constant hum in the background of my life. A reflex honed over years, a silent negotiation of identity that plays out in classrooms, coffee shops, you name it. When you live in, or work in, a predominantly white area, it is almost second nature to mirror the culture that surrounds you.

From the intimate settings of my white friends' homes to the local cycling bar, to networking events, the shift begins the moment I walk into a room where the culture feels...different. My eyes quickly scan the room, and I begin to mirror those around me.

The air crackles with a certain energy—perky, upbeat, a constant hum of enthusiasm. Dialect shifts, word choices morph into 'valley girl' vibes, and the subtle dance of microaggressions begins. It might be a backhanded compliment about my hair, a probing question about my 'mix,' or the casual assumption that I'm an expert on the latest rap song or pop culture. These moments, seemingly small, are constant reminders that I'm navigating a space that wasn't entirely built for me.

That cultural difference I mentioned? I've learned that it can easily be misinterpreted as having an attitude, being standoffish, or being plain rude. This isn't based on a single instance but the cumulative effect of countless interactions. The constant mental calculus of adjusting my tone, my language, my very presence. Out of the fear of being stereotyped or mislabeled is a heavy weight, so the perky mask goes on, even when it feels heavy.

I remember attending an event, surrounded by accomplished women, and I felt the familiar shift. My body language softened, slang disappeared, and my tone became brighter. It wasn't inauthentic, but it was a carefully curated version of myself. In college, where I attended a PWI (predominantly white institute), when making friends, the same dance played out. I wanted to be accepted, not seen as 'the Black girl,' but as simply me.

There's a nervousness, a desire to connect, to make others feel comfortable. At first, the shift feels unnatural, a performance. But over time, it becomes second nature, an altered version of myself that still feels true.

These experiences aren't isolated. Statistics show that even today, schools and professional settings remain largely segregated, even if unintentionally.[1] And the stereotypes that paint people of color in broad, often negative strokes, persist. Knowing this, it's easier to understand why code-switching becomes a survival mechanism. It's a way to bridge the gap, to make others more receptive, to avoid being the 'outcast'. I share this not to place blame but to shed light on a reality many may not fully grasp. It's about understanding the 'why' behind the constant adaptation.

And then there's the tightrope walk of navigating two worlds. The comments, though never explicitly, 'too Black' or 'too white,' are clear: 'Why are you talking like a valley girl?' they'd ask. That translates to: 'Why are you talking like a white girl?'" It was a constant reminder that I was walking a line, never fully fitting in.

But it also sparked a realization: I didn't need to fake it. I could still be myself, even while adapting. I could find my own voice within the code-switching. It forced me to define my own identity, to find the core of who I was, regardless of the environment.

It was never about outright conformity, but about a subtle toning down, a quiet suppression of my true self. The pressure seeped into the very fabric of my personal life, quite literally, impacting even my fashion choices.

I'll never forget the 'grandma chic' comments from my friends in college. Raised by my grandmother, my style leaned towards mature, classic pieces—BCBG, Express, Banana Republic. It wasn't 'grandma,' it was just...me. But in a sea of Fashionnova, Urban

Outfitters, and Nasty Gal, I stood out. And not in a good way, according to them.

I vividly recall the night I was so excited to wear this midi coral bodycon dress from Bebe. It was sooo cute, I thought at least. But my friends quickly corrected me. Their reactions, though well-intentioned, were a reality check. "That's what you're wearing?" they asked, their tone full of concern. "It's cute, but maybe for brunch?"

They found me something more 'appropriate', read: more revealing. It wasn't that they were mean, but it made me feel like I was out of touch. I was confused andddddd a little bit hurt. I started to second-guess my fashion sense. But the peer pressure worked. I started dressing 'sexier,' following trends that didn't always feel authentic. It was a style crisis waiting to happen. This was another form of code-switching, adapting my style to fit the environment.

It was like the chameleon again, shifting colors to blend in but losing sight of its own true hue. My closet became a reflection of this, a chaotic mix of styles that didn't quite align with who I was. It was fun and cute, but it wasn't me.

Thankfully, this didn't lead to major mental health issues, just a prolonged style crisis. But it did affect my self-esteem. I second-guessed my choices, sought external validation, and dressed in ways that didn't feel natural. The real cost wasn't in the clothes I wore but in the energy I spent trying to be someone else.

However, learning to embrace every part of myself has allowed me to be fluid and not feel trapped in a box. I've learned to wear what makes me feel comfortable, confident, and cute. That's all that matters. I stopped seeking external validation, realizing that my opinion was the most important. I get dressed for me.

And now, years later, as a new mom, that journey of rediscovery has taken on a whole new dimension. That's a whole other chapter in itself!

Now, post-grad life has hit me like a tidal wave. A breakup, a 'gap year' that stretched into something entirely different, and a gnawing sense that I was living someone else's life. I was adrift, lost in a sea of confusion and discontent. My body ached, but my spirit? That was where the real tension resided.

It was a visceral feeling: 'This isn't me.' I didn't recognize the reflection staring back. I was broken, stressed, empty, and searching. And so, I embarked on a journey inward, a spiritual quest that led me deeper into my faith and introduced me to the transformative power of mindfulness, meditation, and manifestation—the three Ms, I realized while writing this.

I began to ask the hard questions: What got me here? Where did I want to go? And, most importantly, who did I want to be? What were my core values? How did I want to show up for myself, and for the world, in a way that honored my true self?"

During this time, I rediscovered my love for reading, devouring personal development books like Anna Yusim's book, *Fulfilled*. And as I began to embrace my authentic self, I felt a sense of wholeness, alignment. It wasn't about trying to be someone else; it was about embodying the person I already was, the person I was always meant to be.

This journey of self-discovery wasn't a solitary one. I knew I needed to surround myself with people who would lift me up, challenge me, and celebrate my true self. I became intentional about nurturing relationships with like-minded individuals, people who poured into each other and saw the best in me. I stepped out of my comfort zone, attending local events and connecting with new people. It was awkward at first, but once I made one connection, it opened up a whole new world.

I stopped focusing on superficial qualities and started looking for people with shared values, a growth mindset, and a genuine interest in my well-being. As my habits changed, so did my surroundings. Some people drifted away, while others remained, checking in and offering support. Those who leaned in, who wanted to learn more about my journey, were the ones who truly valued and celebrated my uniqueness.

I learned the power of listening, of asking intentional questions to uncover people's values and beliefs. Through conversations about hobbies, books, and personal development, I found my people— one of those is now my husband.

My advice to others seeking supportive communities is simple: Put yourself out there. Whether it's online or in person, take the first step. Don't be afraid to go to events alone, to step outside your comfort zone. Those uncomfortable moments are where growth and discovery happen.

Finding my tribe has transformed both my personal and professional life. I've found people who see me, know me, love me, and support me, flaws and all. They challenge me to be the best and most authentic version of myself. Personally, it's given me a safe space to be vulnerable and work through challenges. Professionally, it's led to amazing connections, partnerships, and mentorships that have catapulted my success.

As I embraced my authenticity, my self-perception shifted. I realized I didn't have to fit into a single box. I could embrace all facets of myself, tapping into different aspects as needed. Being the 'outcast' became something to celebrate, not hide. My multi-passionate nature, my multifaceted personality was a strength, not a weakness.

I stopped hiding parts of myself and started owning my differences. I still value the ability to connect with others, to make them feel comfortable. But now, it's about blending all my unique elements to show up as the real, true me, not a carefully crafted persona.

To me, owning your voice means owning your truth, your story. It's about expressing your feelings, standing up for your beliefs, and doing so in a way that honors yourself and others. Owning my voice has empowered me to be fully myself, to know what aligns with me and what doesn't. I'm no longer afraid to say no to trends or expectations that don't resonate with my values. It's also made me more empathetic and compassionate, allowing me to connect with others on a deeper level.

Looking back, I realize that being a chameleon was a survival mechanism. I adapted to different environments, wanting to avoid being 'too *insert any stereotypical adjective.*' But I learned that adapting doesn't mean losing yourself. It's about finding a balance, about being comfortable in your own skin, regardless of the situation. And that's what I want for others.

My journey, the one where I learned to navigate different worlds without losing myself, fueled by alignment, self-expression, connection, and purpose, directly shaped the foundation of MG Media Group. My business philosophy is built on values I hold dear: intentionality, creativity, service, personalization, and authenticity. These aren't just buzzwords; they're the guiding principles that infuse every aspect of my work.

My experiences have taught me the profound importance of authenticity, the power of genuine connection, the beauty of individuality, the necessity of empathy, and the strength found in adaptation. These lessons are the rock of how I approach social media strategy. You see, I understand firsthand the emotional toll of suppressing your true self. That's why at MG Media Group, we prioritize helping clients create content that reflects their genuine voice and values. We believe that true connection stems from authenticity, not manufactured personas—because, let's be real, people can always tell when something's off. That's exactly why our services are high-touch services and tailored to each client's unique goals and challenges. Building strong, trusting relationships is paramount. I empower clients to embrace their individuality, express themselves confidently, and overcome the fear of judgment. I help them find their voice.

And because I've learned to adapt, I help my clients navigate the ever-evolving landscape of social media. We believe in ethical and intentional strategies, using social media to build genuine connections, not to manipulate or deceive.

When it comes to creating authentic connections with their audiences, my approach is customer-centric. It's not about shouting about how amazing you are, but rather how your products or services can be transformative, helping clients overcome obstacles and achieve their goals. We really focus on their thoughts, feelings, struggles, dreams, and aspirations rather than just promoting the brand. Focusing on personifying brands, building deeper connections, and developing a sense of community is the core of all of our content strategy, not just pushing sales.

Helping clients express their authentic selves is at the heart of what I do. We start by getting crystal clear on their brand values, how they want to show up for their audience, and the type of content that resonates with them. It's about finding that point where all these elements intersect. I also emphasize the importance of being honest about their capacity. A solopreneur's reality is vastly different from someone with a team, and I want to ensure my clients avoid burnout while still challenging themselves to grow. It's about finding that sweet spot between ambition and sustainability.

My motto is simple: we attract, we don't chase. The goal is to create content with specific messaging so that when someone sees your post, they think, 'This person gets me.' The goal is to make your community feel seen, heard, and understood. When you combine that with your unique value proposition and brand story, you effortlessly draw in your ideal community.

I remember working with a client who felt pressured to create those ubiquitous dancing reels that were all the rage during the pandemic. But it didn't feel authentic to her. I told her, "If it doesn't feel good to you, it won't resonate with your audience." In today's landscape, people can spot inauthenticity a mile away.

Instead, we created content that leveraged trends while staying true to her brand values and her audience's needs. We also used carousels to showcase her expertise. The result? A standout social media presence, consistent posting without burnout, a 300% increase in her email list, boosted podcast downloads, and thousands of new followers. She was able to be herself, and it showed.

My authenticity helps me create a safe space for clients to be themselves, to share their struggles and goals without judgment.

I'm open with them, which encourages them to be open with me. This builds healthy relationships. I also invest time in in-depth audience research, ensuring our content speaks directly to their needs. Helping clients navigate the delicate balance of vulnerability and transparency, sharing their stories in a way that connects without overstepping personal boundaries, is a top priority. This delicate balance is something that took me years to master in my own life, and now I use it as a key tool in authentic social media strategies for the brands I work with.

Using my services means reclaiming your time and peace of mind. No more endlessly scrolling or feeling chained to your phone. No longer will you spend your days working with your own clients and on your business, and nights trying to create viral content. Imagine having hours back in your day, free to focus on what you love. We help to position you as an authority so you attract high-caliber clients. No more guessing, no more chasing algorithms. You'll have a clear content plan that takes the guesswork out of social media, freeing up your time and energy to focus on what truly matters. Say goodbye to never knowing what to post or what to say, or better yet, if your social media efforts will even help you reach your business goals. I transform your social media presence into a powerful growth engine, converting followers into customers and generating real ROI with engaging reels that tell your brand story and uncover hidden opportunities in your strategy.

At MG Media Group, we don't follow cookie-cutter formulas. Every strategy is personalized, taking into account the nuances of your business, your capacity, and the intricacies of your industry and target audience. You don't have to fit into a box; you don't have to dance on reels or share every aspect of your life to be transparent. You can create content that honors who you are while serving your audience. I don't want anyone to sacrifice their true selves for social media. Yes, you might have to step outside your comfort zone, but it should never feel inauthentic.

I now believe my ability to play chameleon, to understand and adapt to different audiences, is a gift. It allows me to help my clients speak to their target audience with authenticity and truth. It's about helping you talk to *your* audience and speak *your* truth while you do it.

So, what's the takeaway here? It's simple: stop worrying so much about how the outside world sees you. Be comfortable in your skin. Find your people, those who make you feel good about yourself, and celebrate every part of you.

Because every part of you is worth being loved and valued. You don't have to fit into anyone's box. You are who you are. Own it. Don't lose yourself, and don't ever sacrifice yourself feeling like you have to be in this box or that box.

EMBRACING ALL OF YOU IS AN
EVOLVING JOURNEY, NOT AN OVERNIGHT
TRANSFORMATION. ONE OF THE BEST THINGS
YOU CAN DO IS SURROUND YOURSELF WITH
PEOPLE WHO ACCEPT YOU AS YOU ARE AND
WHO DON'T ASK YOU TO 'TONE YOURSELF
DOWN' FOR THEIR COMFORT.

I hope you walk away knowing that the right people will accept, love, value, and celebrate every aspect of you—even your flaws. You don't have to put on a mask to hide your insecurities. You don't have to try to be something that you really are not.

Remember, you are enough, just as you are. Embrace your "grandma chic," whatever that means to you! Own your true colors, and watch how the world around you begins to reflect that vibrant authenticity back to you.

ABOUT THE AUTHOR

MORGAN MILLS

SOCIAL MEDIA STRATEGIST & FOUNDER
OF MG MEDIA GROUP

Morgan Mills is a social media strategist and the founder of MG Media Group, a boutique social media marketing agency. As a content creation specialist, Morgan has a deep understanding of organic growth strategies. She leverages the power of social media to achieve exponential business growth for female founders and mompreneurs.

Maximizing each brand's visibility and impact, MG Media Group develops tailored social media strategies that leverage the strength of each platform in tandem with each client's personalized goals. With nearly a decade of experience in social media management, Morgan has a unique ability to create social media strategists that work, content that converts, and growth that lasts.

www.mgmediagroup.org
Instagram: @mg.mediagroup

SIX

WHAT YOU'RE RUNNING FROM IS RUNNING YOU: FINDING FREEDOM IN FAITH AND FLOW

ALESSIA CITRO

"THE CAVE YOU FEAR TO ENTER HOLDS THE TREASURE THAT YOU SEEK." - JOSEPH CAMPBELL

The universe is ever-expanding, and nothing is designed for permanence. It's meant to keep moving. Think of a stream whose flow becomes obstructed. The water stagnates. Mosquitoes breed. Scum collects. It smells terrible. Why? Because it was meant to keep *flowing*. And we too, are meant to flow—always, in all ways. When we don't, we become constipated: energetically, emotionally, spiritually, or intellectually. And just like the stagnant stream, trouble begins to brew within us. It might present as aches and pains, disease, or

69

various forms of dysfunction. Because eventually, everything that's stuck finds its way out, and sometimes the way out is unpleasant.

How apt to open this personal tale of seeking full expression with these illustrations—because another meaning of expression is *release*. It's not just about expressing yourself—it's about getting things out and moving them through! Not only is this essential for our well-being—it's cathartic.

What stands in the way of my own full expression? The barriers boil down to two powerful forces: the fear of others' judgment and the fierce protection of my personal freedom. These fears have kept me from entering the two caves that hold some of my greatest treasures: freedom through structure and, equally important, the full embrace of my Christian faith. What I couldn't see then was how these two fears were actually pointing to the same truth—that sometimes what we resist most is exactly what will set us free.

You may know me as the go-to habits girl, but it wasn't always so. In fact, my relationship status with structure, habits, and routines has been complicated at best and non-existent at worst. I became an expert in it because it's what I needed (and still need) to free myself from the clutches of stuckness and overwhelm.

Something I've been less publicly open about is my faith. As you'll read below, judgment kept me away from God. Even when I found Him again, I struggled to share my faith openly because I couldn't bear to be judged again. Or even worse, to be cast in the same light as the people who tainted my view of what it looked like to be a Christian.

Thanks to divine signs to lean back in, I am finding boundless freedom in my relationship with Jesus. Had it not been for someone else's full expression of faith, I wouldn't have stepped back into His light. And now, I hope to pay it forward to anyone reading this who is grappling with their own faith journey.

As I write a chapter about full expression, please know I'm still navigating these waters myself. Sharing the contents of this chapter isn't comfortable—much of this is quite vulnerable; even raw. But this discomfort is precisely where healing happens. This is the moment when stagnation begins to flow again. And perhaps the most beautiful part of this process? As I release my own dammed-up truths onto these pages, you might feel less alone and find permission to examine what's blocked in your own life. Consider this group therapy through pages—a collective unburdening where my expression might spark yours.

JUDGMENT: THE BARRIER TO AUTHENTIC EXPRESSION

At the root of hesitancy to show up fully is fear of judgment—a poisonous infection that chokes expression. The emotions that judgment creates aren't just uncomfortable—they're visceral and searing, leaving scars that can alter our behavior for decades. We'll construct elaborate defenses to avoid feeling that pain again, even anticipating rejection where none exists. When judged, we experience a cascade of devastation: shame that tells us we're inherently flawed, guilt that we've somehow failed, anger at the injustice of being misunderstood, and grief for the belonging we've lost. And perhaps nowhere is this wound more tender than in matters of faith, where perceived rejection from God and fellow believers cuts deepest, the last place we expect to feel so utterly alone.

You see, until recently, I'd been in an on-again, off-again relationship with God since I was 13 years old. To be clear: it wasn't Him, it was me ... and other Christians that I let keep me from Christ. The first faith fracture happened in 8th grade. I was sitting in the dining room of my best friend's house when I looked out the window and saw her next-door neighbor pounding an election yard sign into the lawn. I asked my friend's parents what it was about. "To vote to ban gay marriage," was their reply. Having an open mind and heart, and not realizing I was in hostile territory, I asked, "But ... so what if they get married?" Their response was nuclear. They erupted, telling me I was a heathen, going to Hell. Those few minutes of judgment kept me away from God for the next 13 years. I wanted *nothing* to do with Christians, Jesus, or a God who would condemn people because of who they loved.

As an adult, it's easy to look at this and think, 'wow, hurt people hurt people,' and those folks had some healing to do. What kind of person would say such a thing, let alone to a child? But when you're 13, you can't zoom out and realize a reaction like this has nothing to do with you. You don't know who you are and feel awkward in your body. You are only beginning to shakily figure out what you believe and what you stand for. And then people within the group that is supposed to be the most accepting and loving of all (Christians) tell you that *you* don't belong? *When you're 13, all you want to do is belong.* And so, rather than feel that pain ever again, you throw the baby out with the bathwater and distance yourself from all of it: from church, from Christians, and worst of all, from a loving God that you hadn't really gotten to know.

Four years later came the next fracture, when I found myself in love for the first time. My high school sweetheart was what you'd call "a good Catholic boy" with a devoutly religious mother. She saw how her son looked at me (trouble), recognized my untamed spirit (double trouble), and to put it bluntly, she detested me.

I could feel her disapproval like a physical weight whenever I entered their home. Her name was Pam, and it wasn't until recently, after writing about the inner critic in my book, *Higher Self Habits*, that I realized something startling. I'd unconsciously named my inner critic after her. The emotional fingerprint of her judgment—that painful experience of being cast as a morally corrupt temptress—has colored my relationship with myself and my faith for decades. Whether her judgment truly stemmed from religious conviction or it was simply my teenage perception doesn't matter—the result was the same. I filed this away as further evidence that I didn't belong in God's family and that He, like Pam, had no place for someone like me.

Despite this rejection, a spiritual longing persisted that I couldn't extinguish. It led me to attend the University of San Diego, a Catholic university, hoping proximity might heal the "church hurt" of my youth. Surrounded by crosses above every doorway and two beautiful churches on campus, I still remained at arm's length from faith. I'd attend mass here and there, but couldn't fully participate in communion or other sacraments since I hadn't been confirmed. The wounds from my youth were still too raw to commit. Yet something beautiful happened during those years—I formed deep friendships with women of faith who have carried me through to this day, including my daughter's godmothers, Shannon and Jackie. These relationships have been a bridge to God throughout adulthood, keeping me connected to spirituality even when formal religion felt inaccessible.

Still, I continued this dance of approach and avoidance, skirting the edges of faith without full commitment, until years later when God would find a way to reach me that no human judgment could obstruct.

DIVINE ENCOUNTERS AND STRUCTURAL BEGINNINGS

If we're open to experiencing it, at some point, each of us will have an encounter with God that transcends all doubt. Mine came at the bedside of my beloved uncle as he took his last breath after battling cancer. The entire family was gathered around his bedside, our hands linked, our voices repeating the Our Father like a sacred heartbeat. As Zio breathed his last, something shifted in the room. I felt the Holy Spirit come and take his soul home. It wasn't just the sudden absence of life in his body. It was a palpable presence; a divine transaction I witnessed with something beyond my five senses. Zio was gone, and he'd had a heavenly escort. In that sacred moment, experiencing the thin space between worlds, I knew I could no longer deny God. The intellectual arguments and emotional barriers I'd constructed gave way. I felt deeply called to discover for myself what it meant to truly know Him.

When this happened, I was a single twenty-six-year-old living in Chicago, partying and living it up. My extracurricular activities were not exactly in line with those of a Godly woman. I'd been feeling a nudge to lean back into faith for many years, but I would shove it down and ignore it. Why even bother if I was so deeply flawed and knew I'd continue to break God's rules? (Turns out that's the whole point.)

But my uncle's passing changed everything. After witnessing his heavenly transition, I committed to getting confirmed as a Catholic at Chicago's historic Old St. Patrick's Church. The confirmation process itself was structured—classes, rituals, requirements—exactly the kind of thing I'd typically resist. Yet something was different this time. I found comfort and solace in the rituals and routine. My heart and the door to a deeper curiosity about structure were cracked open. What if structure isn't to be feared? What if it doesn't eliminate our freedom or expression, but rather, enables it?

This awakening planted a seed, but I still had one foot in each world. Just as I feared that fully surrendering to God would mean losing my identity, I feared that embracing structure would mean sacrificing my spontaneity. What I couldn't see then was how these two journeys—faith and structure—were the two keys to inner peace and freedom. All I needed to do was surrender to this truth.

A significant test of surrender came on the night of my confirmation. Shortly after Zio passed, I met one of the great loves of my life. We'll call him John. By heritage, he was half Catholic, half Jewish and was grappling with his own faith journey. Initially curious about my newfound faith, his reaction during the Easter vigil confirmation mass revealed a fundamental disconnect between us. While I was being anointed with oil at the altar, I looked out and saw him slumped in the pew, visibly uncomfortable and disturbed. Mass ended, and I was flying high on God's glory. But as soon as we left the church, he unloaded on me. He felt like he'd witnessed a cult ritual and declared we would never marry in a church nor baptize our future children. A night of spiritual rebirth became a pivotal crossroads.

A few months later, I knew I had a decision to make. Alone at mass, I got down on my knees, praying fervently for guidance. The answer came immediately—through an elderly couple holding hands in the pew ahead of me, a future I suddenly knew I would never share with John. I heard my Higher Self say loud and clear: "*Everything you want is on the other side of this decision.*" I walked out of Old St. Pat's and ended the relationship, even though it broke my heart.

With nothing left to keep me in Chicago, I moved back home to California. After cycling through rebounds to ease my heartbreak, I had finally had enough. I made the most sincere, passionate prayer of my life: "God, I'm going to abstain from dating to focus on loving *me*. When you know I'm ready—*not when I think I am*—I pray that you'll bring the right man into my life. I pray that you will keep me from missing him when he shows up and from messing it up after he does. Amen."

Two weeks later, I met my incredible husband, Jeff. (Of note, we met on Tinder, which is a longer story for another time, but proof nonetheless that God has a great sense of humor.)

And then, life went on happily ever after . . . until it didn't. Life *was* good. Really good! And I unconsciously began to drift from God as my focus shifted to climbing the corporate ladder. When things are going well, it's easy to take our eyes off God and focus on the material, forgetting that everything here is on loan. Relishing in my good fortune of having a fantastic husband and career, I shelved my identity as a daughter of God in favor of a flimsy identity as a tech sales top performer. In pursuing worldly success and increasing my earnings every year, I lost myself. It's only when we begin to suffer again that we remember we need God and find our way back.

And in due time, I was humbled.

FREEDOM THROUGH SURRENDER

On March 2, 2020, I started my dream job at Google. I was making more money than I ever had and believed I had finally "arrived." My ego was flying high. Then, just a week later, the COVID pandemic hit the US, closing all of Google's offices and my daughter's daycare. Over the next nine months, I watched my career circle the drain as I struggled to tread water and eventually began to drown. A severe depressive episode in December led to medical leave. After returning to work, things briefly looked up, but I was still fundamentally misaligned. It didn't take long before everything began to unravel again.

The only thing flourishing during this time was, ironically, an online wine business that I'd started in late 2019. What began as a fun side hustle grew into a seven-figure success during the pandemic. I was struggling in my corporate role but experiencing great achievement through the wine business success—and numbing the pain with the very product I was selling. I had become dependent on both the accomplishment and the alcohol, neither of which could fill the growing void within.

When my corporate identity crumbled during the pandemic, I found myself stripped of everything I'd been hiding behind. My prestigious job title, my six-figure salary, my carefully constructed image of worldly success—all of it vanished, leaving me face-to-face with two uncomfortable truths:

1. I'd been using career success as a substitute for spiritual connection, and

2. I'd been using alcohol to numb myself to the growing void within.

In my desperation, I finally turned back to God, realizing that what I'd been running from—both divine guidance and aligned structure—were the keys to the freedom I'd been seeking all along. The very caves I'd been avoiding—surrendering to full faith in God and creating aligned structure—were exactly where I needed to enter to find healing.

The initial structure that began to set me free came in the form of boundaries with myself. I had been using alcohol as both shield and sword—protecting me from feeling the full weight of my identity crisis while simultaneously cutting me off from my authentic self. Each glass of wine promised relief from the crushing pressure of mothering a toddler while mourning my professional identity, but delivered only temporary numbness followed by heightened anxiety and shame.

This vicious cycle kept me trapped in a spiritual and emotional purgatory, unable to hear God's voice or my own. When I finally had the courage to face the truth, I discovered that alcohol wasn't enhancing my freedom—it was the very chain keeping me bound.

Through an epiphany that was literally Heaven-sent, I saw the path that alcohol was putting me on. You see, in June of 2022, I had the honor of delivering the joint eulogy for my beloved grandparents. If you were to hear someone describe salt-of-the-earth Midwesterners from the Greatest Generation, Luverne and Anne Marie are the epitome of who you'd imagine. They were kind, hard working, lived in integrity, and were full of love for others, their family, and especially for each other. As I reflected, wrote, and refined a message that attempted to do justice to their collective 195 years of life, I faced my own mortality and had a startling realization.

If I were to die tomorrow, would I like what was said at my funeral, if people were being honest? Or, if I stayed on my current trajectory and lived to be nearly 100 years old like they did, would I have made a positive impact? Would I have been a great wife, mother, sister, and friend? Would I have fulfilled my mission on Spaceship Earth and been who God created me to be?

The answer to all of these questions was a resounding *no*. When I went deeper and kept asking why, the common denominator was alcohol. And so, I made the decision to walk away from my wine business and alcohol altogether. I'm proud to say I'm still alcohol-free, a decision that didn't just improve my health and self-respect, but restored my connection to my higher self and to God. It was the first domino that, when knocked down, began a cascade of healing and self-improvement.

With alcohol out of the way, I had to face a difficult irony. I'd detested corporate structure for years, seeing it as a cage for my creative spirit, only to discover that as an entrepreneur, I needed structure more than ever. Here I was, an ideator who loved trying new things, suddenly realizing that without the external framework of corporate life, I had to create my own container for success. This was the ultimate test—could I create and implement structure, not because someone else required it, but because I chose it for myself?

This breakthrough led to the creation of more intentional and aligned habits. I began to consume books about habits and personal growth—lots of them. As I implemented what I learned with my own twist, I saw that I *was* capable of doing hard things and began to trust myself again. Just as I learned to embrace faith without rigidity, I would eventually learn to embrace structure flexibly and without losing my spark.

One of the personal development books I read during this time introduced me to the concept of cycle syncing. I became very curious about how I could apply the knowledge of my four menstrual cycle phases to my whole life. The books on habits I'd read and learned so much from had helped me make major strides, and yet they were missing something that I hadn't been able to put my finger on. (And, it just so happened that these books were all written by men.)

Suddenly, it clicked. These books offered a masculine perspective that didn't account for an obvious, but often overlooked, biological fact: that men operate on a 24-hour hormone cycle while women operate on a 28-day (ish) hormone cycle. For men, every day is literally *Groundhog Day* from a hormonal perspective. But for us women, well . . . every day is a little different. Is it any wonder, then, that we struggle to do the same thing, day in and day out, as our male counterparts do?

Knowing this, I got curious again. Having experienced the healing power of both spiritual surrender and aligned structure in my own life, I wondered: *What if I could create something that synthesized the feminine energy of flow with the masculine energy of structure? What if the framework I needed didn't exist because I was meant to create it from my own journey of healing and transformation?*

This revelation led to the creation of a framework that honors both our cyclical nature and our need for structure. Because to thrive and be whole, we need both flow and structure, in balance.

Think of structure like a glass, and flow like water. Without the glass, the water spills everywhere, creating chaos instead of nourishment. Without the water, the glass sits empty, all potential but no purpose. But together? Fulfillment. This is what I finally understood: structure isn't the enemy of flow—it's the container that allows it to serve its highest purpose.

THE HIGHER SELF HABITS METHOD™: SPIRITUAL PRINCIPLES IN PRACTICE

Fueled by these insights during my own healing, I discovered what became The Higher Self Habits Method™—a framework that emerged from both behavioral science and my journey back to spiritual wholeness. This method isn't just about getting more done; it's about creating space for what matters most. Each step mirrors a spiritual principle while honoring our unique feminine rhythms:

1. Awareness reflects honest self-examination
2. Alignment echoes our divine purpose
3. Auditing embodies discernment
4. Activation represents aligned action and,
5. Ascension and Amplification celebrate growth and evangelizing your transformation.

Through the example of a habit many of us don't question—drinking alcohol to unwind—let's walk through how the five stages of this method can transform a downward spiral into an upward one:

Aware: Begin by shining a light on what's really happening. Like my own awakening to God's presence at my uncle's bedside, awareness starts with honest recognition. When you notice you're pouring that glass of wine less because you want it and more because you need it to cope with your day, that moment of truth is your first step toward change.

Align: Just as I had to reconcile my spiritual identity with my daily actions, this stage asks you to envision your highest self. For me, this meant facing how my wine business (and the product) was actually keeping me in bondage. Not sure who your Higher Self is? Ask yourself: what would be said at your funeral if you lived your most authentic, masterpiece of a life? When you compare that vision to your current path, the gap becomes clear. That "normal" drinking habit suddenly looks like what it is—a barrier between you and what matters most.

Audit: This is your personal inventory, viewed through Maslow's Hierarchy of Needs. We always want to chase the shiny, sexy goal first... but if you're dehydrated, sleep-deprived, undernourished, or disconnected from basic movement and sunlight, that house of cards will fall down. (I know from experience.) Start with the basics that support your physical well-being—water intake, quality sleep, nourishing food, daily movement, sunlight. For me, this also meant addressing my relationship with alcohol, which was undermining all of these foundational needs. Only when I got honest about how alcohol was affecting my sleep, nutrition, and energy for movement could I create space to rebuild.

Activate: Here's where intention meets action. Every human behavior has four components, which you can remember as ACTS:

- Ambition (desire)
- Capability (ability)
- Trigger (cue)
- Satisfaction (reward)

When I quit drinking, I had to completely redesign my evening routine. I replaced wine with sparkling water and non-alcoholic beer, moved my phone charger out of the bedroom, and created a new wind-down ritual. This supported having a morning that would prime my day for presence and productivity. The secret? Make good habits easier to do while making bad habits harder. The key is engineering your environment to work for and with you. *(Hint: deconstruct the individual elements of a behavior and always focus on making it easier to do.)*

Ascend & Amplify: As you integrate these aligned habits, you'll notice a shift—not just in what you do, but in who you're becoming. You'll experience self-trust, the likes of which you've never known. My sobriety journey became the catalyst for discovering this entire method, showing me how the right habits create space for deeper spiritual connection and a richer life. The radiance others notice in you becomes the evidence of your transformation, just as my daughter now sees me fully present and (mostly) peaceful instead of constantly checking my phone or pouring another glass of wine.

But here's what makes this method truly unique: it's not about forcing yourself into a rigid system. Unlike traditional approaches to habits that expect the same performance every day, this method honors a woman's natural rhythms. Each phase of your cycle brings different strengths—from the creative energy of your follicular phase to the reflective wisdom of your menstrual phase. Just as I learned to work with my body's wisdom instead of against it in sobriety, this framework teaches you to harness your cyclical nature of ebbs and flows rather than fight it.

This is why I advocate for a "morning routine menu" rather than a fixed regimen. Just as your body's needs shift throughout your cycle, your daily practices can flex while maintaining the non-negotiables that support your wellbeing. The structure doesn't confine you—it creates the container that allows your authentic self to flow.

I could write a whole book on this (and did, actually). If creating structure in a way that honors your feminine rhythms intrigues you, be sure to check out the end of this chapter for more information on where and how to go deeper. But beyond the method itself, there's a more profound truth that emerged from this journey.

AUTHENTIC EXPRESSION: YOUR PATH, YOUR WAY

In my resistance to structure, I had been too stubborn to see what now seems obvious: you don't need to be forced into a mold—you get to make your own, flexibly. The way I thought it needed to look—strict, perfectionist, and rigid—was the problem. It wasn't the structure itself, it was my perception of it. And this is why speaking openly about our experiences like this—*fully expressing* what works and what doesn't—is so important: we need to understand and see examples of other people paving their own way so we know, feel, and have the permission to do it *our* way.

CURIOSITY AND COURAGE ARE AN ANTIDOTE.
ARE YOU CURIOUS ENOUGH TO ASK HOW YOU
WOULD OR COULD DO IT DIFFERENTLY? DO
YOU HAVE THE COURAGE TO LOOK WITHIN AND
TAKE ALIGNED ACTION? WHAT IF THE VERY
THING YOU'RE AVOIDING IS THE THING THAT
WILL SET YOU FREE?

The same applies to fully expressing and experiencing what enriches us, in whatever way feels best. Faith is a great example here. In fact, this chapter is a bit like a coming out party for me. Despite the book I wrote having "spiritual" in the subtitle, I didn't mention Jesus at all, and instead of giving God His due, I referenced The Universe. I wish I had owned my full expression of faith while writing that book. But I didn't, for two reasons:

1. I didn't want to be lumped in with the judgmental Christians who wounded me, and
2. I didn't want to be told I was doing it wrong or wasn't Christian enough, and get triggered all over again.

But, full experience leads to full expression, and full expression creates fuller experience. Full experience since writing that book is why you're reading *this* now.

If you also fear judgment around faith, I'd like to offer a profound insight shared with me by a friend who is a student of the Torah and a Messianic Jew (in other words, he is Jewish by birth and faith, and he believes that Jesus is the messiah). In the Jewish faith, there is a principle that you cannot tell another what their relationship with God should look like. In Judaism, there is a concept of *heshbon hanefesh*, or *accounting of the soul*. This accounting is deeply personal, and no one can perform this spiritual self-examination for another. Furthermore, The Mishnah (the earliest codification of Jewish Oral Law) teaches "Do not judge your fellow until you have stood in his place," recognizing that each person's spiritual context is unique.

This wisdom resonates deeply with my own journey. Until December 2024, I was still running my race at arm's length from Jesus—spiritual, yes, but avoiding eye contact with Him, feeling unworthy of such unconditional love.

Through a divine appointment (with one of this book's co-authors, actually), I was led to encounter Him with fresh eyes. While in the back of an Uber, the topic of faith came up. She mentioned that up until recently, she'd only been able to get her business to 90 percent. The missing 10 percent? Jesus.

That moment created a level of clarity that had previously escaped me. My problems in life and business weren't due to a lack of skill or will. They were due to me trying to do it all myself. What if I could trade my hyper-independence (which is the shadow side of being militant about personal freedom, by the way) for surrender? What if I could cast my burdens and worries on Jesus, and instead, simply do my part: faith and aligned action?

My knowing that this conversation was divinely orchestrated was sealed with a sign. My favorite Bible verse—and the only one I had memorized at that point—is Romans 12:2. I mentioned this to her, and she pulled up her sleeve to show me a new tattoo on her arm bearing this exact verse, the content of which is highly relevant here: "Do not conform to the pattern of this world, but be transformed by the renewing of your mind." Is this your sign to renew *your* mind?

Maybe your path of renewal through faith means falling in love with Jesus all over again because of a TV show (which *The Chosen* did for me). Maybe it means posting spiritual insights on Instagram without fear of what the keyboard warriors have to say. Maybe it means worshipping privately in your heart. There is no wrong way to do it. And if someone disagrees, telling you about the speck in your eye, remember—they have a plank in their own.

Remember the metaphor we started with: "The cave you fear to enter holds the treasure that you seek." Don't let fear keep you from entering the cave, whether it's freedom in Christ or freedom through habits. Fear acts as a very convincing bodyguard and does a great job of keeping you safe . . . and the same. Make peace with the fear. Thank it for doing its job. Then go forth with courage and curiosity. What if your full experience and full expression are exactly what will help someone else discover theirs? What if it's exactly what's needed to release the stagnation and restore the flow to your life—and someone else's?

WHERE TO NEXT?

If you're feeling called to explore your own path of authentic expression—whether it's through faith, sharing your message, creating aligned habits, or all of the above—I'd love to support you on that journey.

To learn more about ways we can work together, please visit alessiacitro.com/programs or alessiacitro.com/book to buy my bestselling book, *Higher Self Habits: The Scientific, Strategic, and Spiritual Framework to Get Out of Your Own Way—For Good*. You can also tune into my podcast, *INHABIT with Alessia Citro,* where I explore themes of spirituality, business, and alignment in depth.

Finally, if this chapter resonated with you on a soul level, I'd love to hear about it and connect with you! Send me a message on Instagram at @alessiacitro__.

ALESSIA CITRO

BESTSELLING AUTHOR OF *HIGHER SELF HABITS*, TOP-RANKED PODCAST HOST, AND MENTOR TO EMERGING FEMALE THOUGHT LEADERS

Alessia Citro is a habits expert, transformation coach, and bestselling author who helps women turn everyday habits into unshakable confidence and authentic thought leadership.

Drawing from her own transformative journey—from excelling in tech sales at globally recognized companies like Google and Salesforce to building a 7-figure wine business and embracing sobriety—Alessia empowers visionary women to amplify their voices and step into authority through authorship and podcasting.

She is the creator of the Higher Self Habits Method™, a proven framework blending science, strategy, and spirituality to help women break through limitations and design lives of purpose and impact. Alessia is also the author of Higher Self Habits: The Scientific, Strategic, and Spiritual Framework to Get Out of Your Own Way—For Good and host of the top-ranking podcast INHABIT with Alessia Citro.

www.alessiacitro.com
Instagram: @alessiacitro__

SEVEN

MONEY: THE SELF-CARE PRACTICE THAT FUELS YOUR GENIUS + POWERS YOUR FULL EXPRESSION

ERICA ASH

What if I told you that the biggest act of self-care isn't a spa day, a meditation, or even setting boundaries . . . but your bank account, your cash flow, and your ability to make empowered financial decisions?

What if self-care wasn't just about recovering from stress but removing the root cause of it altogether?

We spend so much energy trying to relax from the stress of running a business, but what if the best way to feel at peace was to stop financial stress before it starts?

The truth is, the thing draining your energy the most isn't your workload or your to-do list.

It's your financial stress.

And that stress is holding you back from being fully expressed in your mission, your impact, and your brilliance.

Think about it. Financial uncertainty is a quiet, constant energy drain.

It's always in the background, always weighing you down.

How much mental space do you waste wondering if you're charging enough?

How many decisions do you put off because you don't trust your numbers?

How much energy do you spend worrying about whether you can afford to hire, invest, or scale?

If you are constantly worried about money, your business is running you—not the other way around.

And the hidden cost of financial stress?

It's stealing your creativity.

It's making you reactive instead of strategic.

It's keeping you in survival mode instead of thriving.

What if money wasn't a source of anxiety but a tool that gave you freedom, peace, and power?

Financial Clarity: The Self-Care We Haven't Been Taught

Right now, for many women and minority business owners, financial clarity feels impossible.

Because let's be honest—the financial system wasn't built for us.

Women-owned businesses:

- Receive less than 3% of venture capital funding.[1]
- Are 80% less likely to apply for grants—even the ones specifically designed for them.[2]
- Fail at a higher rate. Not because they're bad businesses, but because they don't have the same access to capital.

And if you're a woman of color?

- 95% of Hispanic and 68% of Black women entrepreneurs cite lack of access to capital as the #1 reason for closing their business.[3]

It's not a lack of talent that holds women back.

It's not a lack of passion.

It's financial instability that keeps women playing small, draining their genius battery and keeping them stuck in survival mode.

I've seen firsthand how financial instability—and sheer lack of financial clarity—holds even the most impactful businesses back.

When I was leading a nonprofit equine therapy center, we were on a mission to change lives.

The work we did was transformative! We helped veterans heal. We gave children with disabilities confidence. We provided life-changing therapy through the power of horses.

We had the passion.

---

1   Masterson, Victoria. "Women Founders and Venture Capital – Some 2023 Snapshots." *World Economic Forum*, March 2024.

2   Funding Guru. "The Gender Funding Gap – Women More Likely to Receive Business Funding." Funding Guru, February 10, 2023

3   U.S. Securities and Exchange Commission. Access to Capital by Women- and Minority-Owned Businesses. October 2020. https://www.sec.gov/files/oasb-women-minority-businesses-crowdfunding-report.pdf.

We had the community.

But when it came time to expand, we hit a massive roadblock: MONEY.

We needed $4.2 million in capital to complete our facility. We thought we had everything lined up except the bank funding. But when I sat in that boardroom with the bank, I faced a painful reality.

They didn't care about our mission.

They didn't care about the lives we were changing.

They only saw risk.

We only had a surface-level understanding of our financials, and our financials weren't strong enough.

They told us:

"You need more skin in the game."

Translation?

We weren't fundable.

We weren't financially trustworthy.

It didn't matter that we were doing GOOD in the world, we weren't managing our money in a way that gave them confidence in us. We didn't have a clear bread-crumb path showing that we could *handle* the money.

And because of that?

We were delayed for over a year.

We couldn't operate at full capacity.

We left the very people who needed us without access to the programs.

The weight of that financial strain wasn't just on paper, it was on our backs, our minds, and our emotional well-being.

Every single money decision felt like another energy drain. Another roadblock. Another barrier that kept us from focusing on the work that truly mattered.

But here's the thing . . .

We could have done it differently. At the time, I didn't even know what I didn't know. As a new leader at the center, I had inherited a financial sh*it show to say the least.

But here's where the story takes an unexpected turn.

What we were facing wasn't just a funding problem—it was a *financial clarity* problem. And instead of trying to solve it behind closed doors or power through in ashamed silence like so many organizations do, I did something that felt counterintuitive at the time. I leaned into vulnerability.

I encouraged our leadership team to be honest—brutally honest—about where we stood financially. Not just internally, but with our board, our volunteers, and even our larger community. We stopped pretending we had it all together and started asking better questions. We got curious. And that vulnerability, that *willingness to say, "we don't know, but we want to learn,"* was the spark that changed everything.

Financially savvy members of our community stepped up. Donors with business backgrounds came forward not just with money, but with insights, guidance, and connections.

We started to build real business credit instead of relying solely on donations and relationships.

We changed how we talked about funding. We no longer focused exclusively on emotional appeals, but shifted to financially grounded proposals.

We restructured our bookkeeping so it told a clear and compelling financial story. One that built trust with banks, funders, and even ourselves. We dug deeper into grants we'd previously overlooked, simply because we didn't think we'd qualify or we didn't have the language to apply confidently.

It wasn't easy, but it was empowering.

We didn't become financially savvy overnight, but we *were willing to learn*. And that mindset—that shift from pretending to perform to actually pursuing clarity—made all the difference.

But looking back, I know exactly what could have changed our outcome. If we had financial clarity earlier . . .

- We wouldn't have been blindsided in the bank boardroom. Even though we'd been approved for the loan, they weren't going to release the funds until we got our mojo together.
- We would have known exactly where we stood.
- We could have proactively fixed weak financials instead of reacting to rejection.
- We wouldn't have carried the shame of feeling like we were failing—because we would have a plan.

For years, I thought I was practicing self-care.
I set boundaries.
I tried to rest.
I did all the things we're told to do to recharge.
But deep down?
I was still carrying the weight of financial stress.

It followed me into meetings.

It followed me into creative work.

It even followed me into my so-called "rest" time.

I wasn't truly resting.

I was just pausing the panic, until it inevitably returned.

That's when it hit me:

Self-care isn't about what you do to recover from stress.

It's about removing the source of the stress altogether.

So here's the shift . . .

I see this pattern with so many women entrepreneurs.

We invest in our personal growth, in our skills, in our health . . . yet we avoid the one thing that has the biggest impact on our energy, our confidence, and our ability to show up fully: our financial well-being.

When money is uncertain, everything else becomes harder.

You can't focus on growth when your mind is stuck in survival mode.

You can't be strategic when you're scrambling to cover the next bill.

YOU CAN'T FULLY EXPRESS YOUR GENIUS WHEN PART OF YOUR BRAIN IS WHISPERING, *"HOW MUCH LONGER CAN I KEEP THIS UP?"*

That was exactly the struggle we faced at the nonprofit I worked at. We were driven by impact, yet every time we ignored the financial reality of our situation, it didn't just magically go away, it kept creeping back, draining our time, energy, and focus. It wasn't just one financial hurdle, it was a cycle; a constant battle to keep things afloat while also trying to move forward.

And that's exactly what happens to so many business owners. But when you take control of your finances, everything shifts:

- You make decisions from power, not fear. No more saying yes to the wrong clients, underpricing your work, or playing small because you're afraid of where the next dollar will come from.
- You have more energy for the work you love. Financial stress is a slow, steady leak in your energy reserves. Plug that leak, and suddenly, you have the mental and emotional space to be creative, strategic, and visionary again.
- You stop the cycle of feast-or-famine stress. You no longer live in reactive mode, always scrambling to fix the latest financial fire. Instead, you move with confidence, knowing you have a plan and a financial cushion in place.

Money isn't the enemy. It isn't something to fear, avoid, or see as separate from your purpose.

Money is the fuel that lets you show up fully expressed.

It allows you to create freely, serve deeply, and make decisions from a place of confidence instead of desperation.

This isn't about accumulating wealth for wealth's sake.

It's about getting clear on your numbers, so your business stops feeling like a constant "I hope this works" experiment and starts feeling like the powerful, purpose-driven, and profitable venture you set out to build.

3 FINANCIAL SELF-CARE PRACTICES TO START TODAY

(Small shifts that create big emotional and financial freedom.)

1. **Face the Numbers (Stop Letting Your Brain Fill in the Worst-case Scenario)**

   Avoiding your finances doesn't make the stress disappear—it makes it worse. When you sit in uncertainty, your brain fills in the gaps with worst-case scenarios. *"What if I don't have enough?" "What if I'm secretly failing?" "What if I'm missing something huge?"*

   Spoiler: Not knowing is way scarier than the truth.

   When you avoid your numbers, you surrender control. When you look at them, you take it back.

   The simple act of regularly reviewing your numbers builds confidence and clarity, giving you control over your business rather than feeling controlled by it.

   Quick win: Set a 5-minute weekly check-in where you review your bank balance, upcoming expenses, and income projections. No judgment, no panic— just awareness. Because clarity is the first step to empowerment.

2. **Build a 'Genius Fund' (Because Future You Deserves to Breathe Easy)**

   Your Genius Fund is more than just an emergency cushion, it's the safety net that protects your creativity, your confidence, and your ability to make bold moves in business.

   This fund isn't just for disasters, it's for keeping you out of financial fight-or-flight. It ensures that when life happens (because it will), you're prepared, not panicked. Keeping this money in a separate business savings account means it's accessible but not easy to dip into for everyday spending.

   Quick win: Open a dedicated savings account under your business and transfer $20 to start. No amount is too small, what matters is the habit. Small, consistent deposits build financial resilience faster than you think.

3. **Set a CEO Payday (Because You Are Not Your Business's Last Priority)**

   One of the biggest mindset shifts in business is realizing that you are not just the worker, you are the CEO.

   Too often, business owners reinvest every dollar back into the business, waiting for a future "someday" to finally pay themselves. But if you don't set the precedent now, when will you?

Paying yourself consistently—even if it's a small amount at first—reaffirms that you are running a real business, not a side hustle or a passion project.

It shifts your mindset from scrambling to stability, from scarcity to ownership. And it forces you to structure your finances in a way that supports long-term sustainability rather than constantly operating in feast-or-famine mode.

Your paycheck isn't just a reward—it's a declaration: *I am building a business that supports me.*

Quick win: Transfer a meaningful amount from your business to your personal account today—whether it's $50 or $500. Mark it as an owner distribution, and commit to making it a recurring payday, even if you start small.

WHY THESE SMALL SHIFTS MATTER

None of these steps require a massive overhaul. They're simple, powerful habits that build confidence, reduce stress, and shift you into the CEO role you're meant to be in.

Because financial clarity = financial confidence.

And real self-care isn't escaping financial stress, it's eliminating it.

Most of us were never taught how to manage money in a way that feels empowering. In a true recharge, self-care kind of way. But that changes today.

You don't need more willpower. You need a financial foundation that lets you thrive. Because real self-care isn't about escaping stress, it's about building a life where you don't have to. And when you do that, you can show up fully expressed, operating from your genius and making the impact you were meant to make.

If this stirred something in you—if you're ready to release financial stress and reclaim your energy so you can show up fully expressed in your life and business—I'd love to support you.

To take the first step, grab my free Financial Self-Care Starter Kit: 3 Simple Steps to Reclaim Your Peace and Power. Over three short emails I'll help you create more clarity, stability, and confidence with your money. Sign up at https://fundhercapital. myflodesk.com/selfcarestarterkit and start feeling financially empowered. One simple habit at a time.

You can also explore my courses, coaching, and resources at fundhercapital.com which is designed to help women business owners build financial trust, get fundable, and finally feel at peace with their numbers.

And if this chapter resonated with you, come say hi! Message me on Instagram at @fundher_capital I'd love to hear what landed, what you're shifting, or how you're reclaiming your financial power.

ABOUT THE AUTHOR

ERICA ASH

FOUNDER OF FUNDHER CAPITAL

Erica Ash is the founder of FundHER Capital which helps female founders uplift their financial literacy, feel confident in their business finances, and scale sustainably. Providing education on grants and business credit for female entrepreneurs, Erica uses her F.L.I.G.H.T framework to help founders build financial foundations and utilize key financial tools for growth. Erica teaches founders how to make financial clarity a habit not a stressful task, showing women how the power of small, consistent actions build wealth.

www.fundhercapital.com/
Instagram: @fundher_Capital

EIGHT

BREAKING THE SILENCE: HOW MIDWIVES ARE SAVING LIVES IN A SYSTEM THAT'S FAILING MOTHERS

MELISSA DEAN

As a midwife, I have had the incredible honor of walking alongside families during one of the most transformative moments of their lives—bringing a baby into this world. I've held the hands of women as they labor through contractions, whispered words of encouragement when they thought they couldn't do it anymore, and celebrated with them as they triumphantly brought life earthside.

I've also wiped away tears of fear and frustration as women navigate a system that far too often does not listen, does not honor their needs, and sometimes doesn't protect their lives. And while I cherish every beautiful birth story I've been part of, I cannot stay silent about the dark reality that every five days in California, a mother dies from pregnancy-related complications. [4]

Let that sink in. Every week, somewhere in our state, a family is left without a mother, a baby left without a nurturing touch, partners left grieving, and children growing up without the person who should have been there to watch them grow.

What makes this even harder to swallow is knowing that the vast majority of these deaths are preventable. We have the knowledge, we have the tools, and yet women—especially women of color—continue to die because of failures in care, systemic racism, and a healthcare model that prioritizes profit over people.

And while California's maternal mortality ratio is lower than the national average, it is still rising.[5] This is supposed to be one of the most progressive, advanced healthcare systems in the world—yet women continue to die at rates two to three times higher than women in countries like the Netherlands and the United Kingdom, where midwives serve as primary care providers for pregnancy and birth.

Our national crisis is even worse. The United States has the highest maternal mortality rate among all wealthy, developed nations. In a country that spends more on healthcare per capita than any other nation on earth, we are failing our mothers. Women are more likely to die from pregnancy or childbirth here than in any other high-income country—and the risk is only growing.[6]

---

4   "Pregnancy Mortality Surveillance System." *Maternal Mortality Prevention*, 14 Nov. 2024, www.cdc. gov/maternal-mortality/php/pregnancy-mortality-surveillance/?CDC_AAref_Val=https:// ww.cdc.gov/reproductivehealth/maternal-mortality/pregnancy-mortality-surveillance-system. htm.

5   Department of Public Health. *Pregnancy-Related Mortality*. www.cdph.ca.gov/Programs/CFH/ DMCAH/surveillance/Pages/Pregnancy-Related-Mortality.aspx.

6   Tikkanen, R., Gunja, M. Z., FitzGerald, M., & Zephyrin, L. (2020). *Maternal mortality and maternity care in the United States compared to 10 other developed countries*. The Commonwealth Fund. https://www.commonwealthfund.org/publications/issue-briefs/2020/nov/maternal-mortality-maternity-care-us-compared-10-countries

But not everyone bears this burden equally. Black women are three to four times more likely to die from pregnancy-related complications than white women, even when they have higher levels of education, higher income, and good insurance coverage.[7] American Indian/Alaska Native and Pacific Islander women are also at much greater risk. It doesn't matter how prepared, educated, or resourced a woman is—the color of her skin often determines the care she receives, or worse, doesn't receive.

These are the women I fight for.

I've seen the difference it makes when a mother has a midwife by her side—someone who listens, who knows her story, who stays with her for the long haul. I know in my bones that midwives save lives. But we can't keep doing this life-saving work if we aren't paid enough by insurance to keep our doors open.

This isn't just a healthcare issue. It's a human rights issue. It's an issue of racial justice, of economic justice, and of moral responsibility. We can do better. We must do better.

In the following pages, I will share with you the data, the stories, and the solutions—the reasons why midwifery care is the key to turning this healthcare and human rights crisis around. I hope that by the time you finish reading, you will not only feel informed, but compelled to act.

Because mothers—and their babies—deserve nothing less.

---

7   Centers for Disease Control and Prevention. (2019). *Racial and ethnic disparities continue in pregnancy-related deaths*. U.S. Department of Health and Human Services. https://www.cdc.gov/media/releases/2019/p0905-racial-ethnic-disparities-pregnancy-deaths.html

I. MIDWIFERY CARE: WHAT IT LOOKS LIKE AND WHY IT SAVES LIVES

Midwifery care is relationship-based, individualized, and grounded in evidence. In my practice, prenatal visits are not rushed 10-minute check-ins. They are full conversations—often an hour long—where we discuss nutrition, emotional well-being, trauma history, birth preferences, and fears. I take the time to know my clients deeply because I know that trust and understanding are critical to safe care.

When labor starts, I come when they call, and I stay until their baby is in their arms, whether that takes 6 hours or 24. I'm not leaving to catch another baby down the hall. I'm there, holding their hand, providing support, helping them breathe through contractions. I am also providing careful clinical monitoring. I don't leave them alone in a hospital room to wait for a nurse to come back. I stay, because being present is part of how we save lives.

Postpartum, I visit mothers at home checking not only the baby but the mother's body, mind, and heart. I help with breastfeeding, screen for postpartum depression, and assess healing. This is holistic care, and it makes a difference—especially for those at heightened risk of falling through the cracks of a fragmented system.

Midwives are also trained to practice trauma-informed care—which means asking permission before every touch, respecting boundaries, and creating a sense of safety and control. For women who have survived sexual violence, this approach can mean the difference between a retraumatizing birth and an empowering one. This type of care is life changing for these women.

II. HOSPITAL VS. MIDWIFE CARE: A SYSTEM THAT REWARDS WHAT HARMS, AND IGNORES WHAT HEALS

For over a decade, I have seen the stark contrast between midwifery care and hospital-based obstetric care. Midwives offer care that centers on trust, respect, and collaboration. Hospitals, as they are currently structured, often center on efficiency, profit, and liability avoidance.

Let me share the numbers: 33% of hospital births end in cesarean section—a major abdominal surgery that carries serious risks, including hemorrhage, infection, increased risk of complications in future pregnancies, and long-term impacts on maternal health. In midwife-led birth centers, the cesarean rate is closer to 6%, without increasing risks to mothers or babies.

And yet, the system rewards hospitals for these surgeries. Doctors are paid thousands for birth care, which often amounts to a handful of short prenatal visits and showing up to catch the baby. Midwives, who spend dozens of hours providing thorough, holistic care, are paid about $2,000 under Medi-Cal. When you break this down, doctors are effectively paid $1,857 an hour, while midwives are paid about $59 an hour.

Midwives like me pour our heart and soul into this work, but the math doesn't add up—and it's driving many out of practice. Since 2020, 25 birth centers have closed in California alone, leading to an increase in maternal care deserts, or areas where mothers are unable to receive sufficient care within a safe distance.[8] Numbers across the U.S. are equally as high. This is 100% due to the inability to obtain sustainable insurance contracts from insurance

---

8   Hwang, Kristen. "California Birth Centers Are Shutting Down. A Lawmaker Has a New Plan to Help Them." *CalMatters*, 2 Dec. 2024, calmatters.org/health/2024/12/birth-center-licensing-bill.

companies. We can't afford to be there for the women who need us most if insurance companies won't fairly cover the costs of running our practices.

And when midwives can't practice, families are left with no other option but hospital births, where their risks of trauma and complications skyrocket.

But this isn't just about fairness. It's about outcomes—and money. Cesarean births are expensive, not only for the surgery itself but for the long-term complications they can create: NICU stays, maternal rehospitalizations, and future pregnancy risks. The Strong Start for Mothers and Newborns Initiative, led by the Centers for Medicare and Medicaid, showed that midwifery care reduces preterm births, low birth weight, and other costly complications.

Investing in midwifery care saves lives, and saves money.

What's more, we now know that cesarean birth can disrupt the baby's microbiome, setting them up for higher risks of asthma, allergies, obesity, and autoimmune diseases later in life. Babies born vaginally are inoculated with beneficial bacteria as they pass through the birth canal, bacteria that help shape a healthy gut microbiome. When cesareans are performed unnecessarily, we deprive babies of this vital start in life.

REAL STORIES: MOTHERS WHO DESERVED BETTER

I've cared for women who came to me after traumatic hospital births where they were coerced into interventions, yelled at, or left alone. Women who had lost trust in their bodies because of the way they were treated—not as individuals, but as cases to be managed. I have seen the deep wounds that birth trauma leaves behind.

One mother, after a violent and dehumanizing first birth in a hospital, came to me determined to write a different story. Through our work together, she birthed her baby gently, surrounded by love and safety. Afterward, she said, *"I didn't think I could do this. You believed in me when I didn't believe in myself."*

In recent headline news there are far too many stories like Kira Dixon Johnson's—a healthy, educated Black woman who died from an untreated postpartum hemorrhage after her husband's desperate pleas for help were ignored. Or Shalon Irving—a CDC epidemiologist who died weeks after birth from complications that her providers brushed off. If these women, with every possible resource, could not be saved, what hope do women in marginalized communities have?

One such woman was Tatia Oden French, a vibrant, accomplished Black woman whose life was cut short during childbirth. Tatia, who was highly educated and in excellent health, trusted the medical system to guide her safely through delivery. Instead, she was treated with off label medications that were not fully explained, and both she and her baby lost their lives. Her husband and parents were left to carry on without her in their lives. Stories like hers illuminate the deep failures in maternal care—how hospitals often cause the complications that arise, and how Black women's complications are often dismissed or minimized.

Even Serena Williams, one of the most famous and powerful women in the world, was nearly a statistic. After delivering her daughter via cesarean section, Serena immediately recognized the signs of a life-threatening pulmonary embolism—something she had experienced before.

She repeatedly told her healthcare team that she needed a CT scan and heparin to prevent clotting. But instead of listening, her nurses dismissed her concerns. It was only after she pushed relentlessly and demanded further care that doctors finally realized she was, in fact, experiencing a severe embolism. Had she not been able to advocate for herself with such persistence, she may not be here today

If Serena Williams—an Olympic champion with access to the best healthcare in the world—was ignored, what does that say for the everyday Black woman who walks into a hospital to give birth?

The fear and distrust that many Black women feel toward the medical system is not irrational, it is built on generations of lived experience. They have seen their mothers, sisters, and friends suffer unnecessary trauma. They have read the statistics and know the risks. They have seen too many women ignored when their pain is real, their fears justified, and their lives hanging in the balance.

We must demand better. For Kira, for Shalon, for Tatia. For Serena. And for the millions of unheard women who do not have the platform to make their stories known. For every mother who walks into a hospital wondering if she will walk back out.

Midwifery care is not a privilege. It is a necessity. And it is time for the system to recognize that before more lives are lost.

III. THE COST OF IGNORING MIDWIVES

What is the real cost of ignoring midwives? It's counted not only in dollars but in lives lost, families broken, and futures destroyed.

EVERY TIME A WOMAN DIES IN CHILDBIRTH, WE LOSE A MOTHER, A DAUGHTER, A PARTNER, A PROFESSIONAL, AND A COMMUNITY MEMBER. AND BEYOND THE LIVES LOST, THE FINANCIAL TOLL ON OUR HEALTHCARE SYSTEM IS STAGGERING.

Cesarean sections, for example, are not only costly in the moment—totaling as much as $30,000 to $40,000 per birth, to sometimes 5 times that number—but they also increase risks in future pregnancies: placenta previa, placenta accreta, uterine rupture, and more life threatening surgical complications.[9] NICU admissions, which are much higher in hospital births, can add tens of thousands of dollars to the cost of delivery. And when birth is traumatic, postpartum depression and PTSD can follow—leading to further medical expenses and lost productivity for families and employers.

Yet, while hospital-based birth and high-intervention models rack up these costs, midwifery care has been shown to significantly reduce cesarean rates, NICU admissions, and maternal complications. According to the Strong Start for Mothers and Newborns Initiative, women cared for under midwifery-led models were more

---

9   *Health costs associated with pregnancy, childbirth, and postpartum care - Peterson-KFF Health System Tracker*. (2024, July 8). Peterson-KFF Health System Tracker. https://www. healthsystemtracker.org/brief/health-costs-associated-with-pregnancy-childbirth-and-postpartum-care/#:~:text=However%2C%20while%20the%20average%20total,a%20vaginal%20delivery%20($2%2C655

likely to carry pregnancies to term, had fewer preterm births, and better outcomes overall—while costing Medicaid substantially less.

Still, insurance companies continue to deny midwives fair reimbursement, paying midwives a fraction of what obstetricians receive for care that is longer, deeper, and more relationship-based. Despite the plethora of data supporting midwifery care, birth centers across the country struggle to meet ends meet. Every time a birth center closes, families lose a critical option. Families are forced back into hospital systems where their choices are limited, where they face higher risks of unnecessary interventions, and where marginalized voices are least likely to be heard.

The costs of midwifery care are not measured in just dollars in and dollars out, the personalized experience of working with a midwife is also measured in the emotional toll on midwives themselves—many of whom have dedicated their lives to serving women. Most of us enter this work not for financial gain or prestige, but because we feel deeply called to care, to support, to stand beside women during one of the most transformative times of their lives. We carry the stories of each birth, each family, each sacred moment—and also the trauma, the fear, and sometimes the grief.

We are up all night birthing mothers, then back to the clinic the next morning. We hold space for joy and sorrow, strength and vulnerability. But after the birth is over, we return not just to charting, breastfeeding support, new mother support, and follow-up visits, but to battles with insurance companies, fighting to get paid for the care we've already given with our whole hearts. Many of us spend hours every week navigating denials, underpayments, and delays, all while struggling to keep our practices financially viable.

This work, while meaningful, takes a physical and emotional toll. The burnout is real. The stress of staying afloat in a system that undervalues us wears on our bodies, our minds, and our families. Some midwives leave the profession not because they want to, but because they can no longer afford to stay.

When we ignore midwives, we are perpetuating a system that makes birth dangerous and expensive—a system where families suffer, midwives disappear, and healthcare costs skyrocket. This is a crisis we can no longer afford to ignore.

IV. HOW YOU CAN HELP

So where do we go from here? We know what works. Midwifery care saves lives. The studies show it. The stories of countless mothers across the world demonstrate it. Midwifery care provides culturally competent, trauma-informed, respectful care that keeps mothers and babies safe and well. But unless we act, this care will remain out of reach for most women.

Here's what we need—and how you can help:

1. DEMAND FAIR REIMBURSEMENT FOR MIDWIVES

Insurance companies, including Medi-Cal, must pay midwives fairly for the life-saving, intensive care they provide. Midwifery care should not be a luxury for only those who can pay out of pocket—it should be a basic, accessible right for every family. Call your legislators. Write letters. Attend hearings. Tell them that mothers and babies deserve better.

2. SUPPORT BIRTH CENTERS AND MIDWIFERY PRACTICES

Birth centers are closing because the system is unsustainable. If you can, donate to birth centers, support community midwives, and advocate for funding programs that keep them open. Help ensure that families have options outside of the hospital system.

We know that midwives save lives. We know that midwives reduce C-sections, prevent complications, and give families the care they deserve. But if we don't demand that insurance companies pay midwives fairly, this option will disappear—and mothers will keep dying.

3. EDUCATE AND SHARE THE TRUTH

Many people still don't know the depth of the maternal health crisis in the U.S. They don't realize that the U.S. has one of the highest maternal mortality rates among wealthy nations, or that midwives are key to turning this around. Share this knowledge. Talk to your friends, family, and communities. Make maternal health part of the public conversation.

4. CHOOSE MIDWIFERY CARE AND ADVOCATE FOR YOURSELF

If you are pregnant or planning to be, explore midwifery care as a safe and powerful option. And whether you choose a midwife or not, know your rights, ask questions, and insist on respectful care. Hire a doula to be by your side to help you advocate for yourself. You deserve to be heard, seen, and cared for as a whole person—not just a patient.

5. HOLD SYSTEMS ACCOUNTABLE

Hospitals, insurance companies, and policymakers need to hear directly from families impacted by this system. If you or someone you love has been harmed by preventable birth trauma, tell your story. Share it with legislators, on social media, and in advocacy groups. Change comes when the human cost becomes impossible to ignore.

FINAL WORDS: FOR EVERY MOTHER AND BABY

Behind every statistic is a mother who should still be here. A baby who should be growing up in their mother's arms. A family that should be whole.

I have held women as they cried from fear, from trauma, from the joy of healing after a gentle birth. I have looked into the eyes of mothers who survived birth against all odds—and I have mourned those who didn't. These experiences are what drive me to write this and to call on all of us to stand up and demand better.

We don't have to accept the current state of maternal health in this country. We can choose to value women's lives, to honor birth as sacred and transformative, and to support the midwives who are holding that vision every day.

We can create a world where mothers are safe, where babies are born into love and care, and where families thrive.

But only if we act—and we must act now.

If you are reading this, you are part of this movement. You can help save mothers and babies. You can be part of making birth safe, joyful, and sacred again.

Will you join me? You can follow me @casanatalbirthcenter or @midwife-Melissa-Dean.

ABOUT THE AUTHOR

MELISSA DEAN

MIDWIFE, MATERNAL CARE ADVOCATE AND FOUNDER OF CASA NATAL BIRTH AND WELLNESS CENTER

Melissa Dean is a midwife and the founder of Casa Natal Birth and Wellness Center and the Vice President of the California Chapter of the America Associate of Birth Centers. In 2024, Casa Natal was voted the Best birth center in the Bay Area by Bay Area Parents. As a functional and integrative medicine practitioner, Melissa combines her expertise in women's health with her midwife practice. She provides care with an emphasis on holistic health modalities to bring wellness to women in every stage of their health: including preconception, childbirth, transition to motherhood and beyond.

Melissa's expertise has been featured in leading publications such as The Bump, Today's Parent, Patient, InHealth and The CheckUp. She has been a featured guest on leading podcasts such as Dear Doula, Sparking Wholeness, The Hypnobirthing Podcast, Papaya Health, The Freely Rooted Mama.

www.casa-natal.com
Instagram: @casanatalbirthcenter, @midwife-Melissa-Dean

NINE

WHEN THE UNIVERSE MAKES YOU STOP AND LISTEN

SUSAN COOLEY

"Who do you think you are?"

I've heard this question many times—sometimes whispered in doubt, other times hurled like a challenge. But the most powerful moment came when I asked it of myself, not just from insecurity but from curiosity.

Who do I think I am? And why have I spent so much of my life waiting for someone else to answer that for me?

For years, people have described me in contradictory ways:

Shy. Outspoken.

Too much. Not enough.

Selfish. Generous.

Difficult. Easygoing.

It seemed who I was depended entirely on who was looking.

But the words that stuck the most were the ones that felt like expectations: responsible, reliable, hardworking. The one who always shows up.

I wore those words like armor, believing they defined me.

But what happens when all of that is stripped away?

Who am I, then?

A TIME I WAS NOT FULLY EXPRESSED

As the fourth of five children, I learned to navigate life in the middle. Not the oldest, not the youngest—I wasn't the one setting the rules or being doted on. I was just . . . there. I figured out how to be low maintenance, independent, and capable because that's what seemed to work.

But school was different.

Catholic school had rules, order, and clear expectations. There was right and wrong. Black and white. Do the work. Follow the structure. Stay in line.

I learned quickly that being responsible and self-sufficient was rewarded. I wasn't the kid who needed much, so I lived up to that expectation. I didn't ask for more. I just did what was expected—and I did it well.

And for most of my life, that was enough.

As I got older, I'd occasionally wonder if there was something more. Logically, I knew there had to be. But I never really believed it for myself. The idea of something beyond my daily life felt too big, too uncertain. I didn't even know where to start—so I didn't.

Then, my Achilles heel injury happened. And as I lay there, I had a thought I couldn't ignore:

I think the universe is trying to tell me something.

HOW WORK BECAME MY IDENTITY

For as long as I can remember, I have taken pride in my work ethic. I was the person who could handle anything. Who didn't let stress slow her down. Who kept going no matter what.

People respected me for it.

But beneath the surface, I was living out of alignment. And because I wouldn't slow down on my own, life had to hit me over the head to get me to stop.

MY NORMAL DAY

My day started around 5:15 a.m. with coffee, stretching, and the gym—a sacred hour of uninterrupted "me time." At the time, I wouldn't have called it mindful. It just felt good because no one else needed anything from me yet.

But the moment I returned home, everything shifted. Calm evaporated into chaos: quick shower, hurried skincare, racing to the car. Emails and texts already waiting: "When are you coming in?"

One morning, distracted by work, a dog darted in front of my car. I hit the brakes—but not in time. Horrified, I slammed the car into park and jumped out, shaking and in tears. I rushed to the dog's owner, asking if he was okay. Thankfully, she reassured me he was—but my heart still raced, and I stood there overwhelmed with relief and emotion. Moments later, I was back in the car, and by the time I arrived at work, it had already faded into the background noise of the day.

Another Saturday, running late after an unexpected work call, I tripped and fell into a metal hamper. A missing cap on one of the rods punctured my leg. Blood poured down. I wrapped towels around it, ignored the pain, made it to two appointments, and then finally drove myself to urgent care. Thirteen stitches.

Even then, I didn't stop. Chaos had become my baseline. I believed that's what responsible, successful people did.

THE BREAKING POINT – MY BODY FORCED ME TO STOP

It was 6:55 a.m., the last move of my morning workout. Toe taps on a bench—a motion I'd done hundreds of times before.

And then—POP.

A sound like a gunshot.

My foot collapsed under me. No pain, just silence. It felt disconnected, like it no longer belonged to me.

People rushed over. Someone asked if I was okay. But my mind was on work:

What about my calls today? My laptop? Our Europe trip?

My husband carried me out of the gym. I couldn't walk—not from pain, but because my body had shut down.

Even then, I had him carry me to my desk so I could log into work.

Because who was I if I wasn't productive? If I wasn't the one who always showed up?

That was the moment I realized: I had tied my worth to my ability to perform.

And now, I had no choice but to stop.

HOW SKINCARE BECAME MY SANCTUARY

When I couldn't move freely, I had no choice but to sit still—and for the first time, I realized how much I had been using movement, work, and noise to avoid myself.

In that stillness, skincare became something more than a routine. It became a ritual. A form of expression when I couldn't do anything else. Each step was a deliberate act of care—not because I had somewhere to be but because I finally had nowhere to run.

At first, it was about comfort. The scent of a cleanser. The warmth of a towel. The simple act of doing something gentle in a moment when I felt anything but strong.

But slowly, it became something deeper. A way to reclaim my body, my time, and my worth. A message to myself: I matter, even when I'm not performing.

It was the first time I let something be just for me—and that was revolutionary.

FROM RITUAL TO VISION

What started as survival slowly became a sacred pause—and eventually, a calling.

THE MORE I ALLOWED MYSELF TO BE STILL, THE MORE I HEARD THE WHISPERS OF SOMETHING NEW. A VISION ROOTED NOT IN PRODUCTIVITY BUT IN PRESENCE. IN BEAUTY. IN INTENTION. I DIDN'T KNOW IT YET, BUT THIS WAS THE BEGINNING OF FINNY RUTE.

THE HEALING JOURNEY - LEARNING A NEW DEFINITION OF STRENGTH

Healing wasn't just about my Achilles—it was about unlearning what strength meant.

I slowed down. I let myself rest. I stopped forcing my body to push through.

And in that stillness, I asked questions I had never given myself space to ask:

What if strength isn't about endurance—but about alignment?

What if I stopped trying to prove my worth and started trusting it?

Who am I if I'm not working myself to exhaustion?

I didn't have the answers.

But I knew I was done living the old way.

Before my injury, my time didn't feel like it belonged to me. I had convinced myself that slowing down wasn't an option. Boundaries felt like a luxury I couldn't afford. I was so focused on staying ahead of the next demand that I rarely stopped to ask if any of it felt right.

Now, I approach my time differently. I take breaks without guilt. I meditate in the mornings—or even in the middle of the day if I need it. I listen to calming music or sit in silence. I give myself space to be present.

What's changed isn't just my schedule—it's my mindset.

I no longer equate nonstop motion with strength.

I trust that I'm capable—and I don't have to exhaust myself to prove it.

SEEKING OUT EXPANDERS - FINDING THE WOMEN WHO SHOWED ME WHAT WAS POSSIBLE

At first, I felt like I was floating in limbo.

I knew I wanted a different life, but I didn't have a roadmap.

So I started seeking it out.

I joined masterminds, online communities, Instagram spaces, and courses. I found mentors who had built what I longed for.

And I started realizing—

If I admire something in someone else, it already exists within me.

STEPPING INTO FULL EXPRESSION

When I stopped trying to earn my worth through output, I started wondering what I might create simply because I wanted to.

No more waiting for permission.

I launched Finny Rute—a brand built on self-expression and intention.

A year before, I would never have believed I could create something of my own. But now? I claimed it.

My injury was deeply transformative—not just physically but emotionally and spiritually. During recovery, skincare and mindful practices allowed me to reclaim my sense of self-worth and joy.

When creating Finny Rute, I thought, "If I can share even a fraction of these insights with other women, it would be incredible." I wanted luxurious products that allowed women to take care of themselves without adding pressure to their already full plates. Each product is intended to feel luxurious, smell divine, and genuinely do good—adding intentional, nourishing moments into daily life.

Finny Rute is more than a brand.

It's an embodiment of mindful self-care, intuitive wellness, and intentional beauty.

Because when you take time to care for yourself with intention, it doesn't just transform how you feel—it leaves you glowing from the inside out. So your authentic beauty can shine without apology.

WHAT I LEARNED - LESSONS FROM THIS JOURNEY

You don't have to earn your worth. You are already enough.

Rest is not weakness. Pushing through is not strength.

What you admire in others is a reflection of what's inside of you.

STEP INTO YOUR FULL EXPRESSION

JOURNAL PROMPTS:

- Where in your life are you still performing instead of being?
- If you weren't proving anything to anyone, how would you live differently?

NEXT STEP:

For the next 7 days, commit to one small act of full expression—whether it's setting a boundary, speaking up, or doing something just because it lights you up.

"Who do you think you are?"
The answer isn't something you need to earn.
It's something you already are.
It's time to own it.

ABOUT THE AUTHOR

SUSAN COOLEY

FOUNDER OF FINNY RUTE

Susan Cooley's journey to founding Finny Rute began at an uncertain time in her life. Health challenges had left her unable to walk for almost a year and an unexpected career shift occurred soon thereafter. However, in a time of uncertainty, she found solace in a simple but powerful daily ritual: her skincare routine.

This small act of self-care became her source of strength at a time when she needed it the most. She became grounded in her routine and was able to reconnect with herself. Through this transformation, Susan discovered that skincare was more than just a way to achieve healthy skin; it was a tool for resilience, self-reliance, and inner confidence. More than just skincare, Finny Rute is about nurturing both the skin and the soul, offering products that encourage reflection, growth, and self-care.

Susan believes that beauty is not just about appearance; it's about how we feel and the journey we take to become our best selves. With Finny Rute, she invites others to embrace their own rituals, reconnect with themselves, and find self-confidence from within.

www.finnyrute.co
Instagram: @finnyrute

TEN

SECRETS TO LIVING FINANCIALLY FULLY EXPRESSED

SHALAREE LAMBOY

What truly delights you? What lights you up? For me, it's exploring Gothic cobblestone streets in Barcelona, taking in the 360 degree view of Rome from atop the Colosseum, or eating fresh fish at a restaurant on the Amalfi coast. It's making memories with the people I cherish, laughing uncontrollably until my eyes leak and I can't catch my breath. I also desire that these precious experiences continue for my family after I'm gone (many, many years from now!) This means saving to create generational wealth that lasts longer than I do. This seemingly creates a strange dichotomy: the two things I want most, are polar opposites.

The other thing that deeply delights me is having certainty and control around my financial future. I used to believe it was a choice between the independence to fully and freely live life right now, or planning like a responsible adult for my family's financial future. I was hoping to create significance and legacy that punctuates life like a happy exclamation mark, all while enjoying my own life. Have you ever struggled with the urge to embrace the "YOLO" philosophy and just do *everything* because "you only live once" while still hoping to build lasting wealth for your family? Then, this might be for you. I promise, there is a simple way to have both. It just took me the long way around to get there so you don't have to. But first, let's go back to the beginning so you can get a better sense of how I was able to come across this best kept secret.

Watching PBS with my two-year-old, my hubby and I saw Rick Steves hiking the Cinque Terre, five oceanfront hill towns connected by hiking trails, boats, and trains in Italy. We looked at each other and said, "Let's go!" We had never been to Europe, and hiking the Cinque Terre became our new dream.

Even though we were making good money, and we were doing all the typical financial things such as contributing to our 401k, owning investment real estate, and investing in the market with a financial advisor, there never seemed to be the right time to divert money from our long-term goals to go hike Cinque Terre. And it remained our dream for almost 10 years.

Postponing our dream gave me a realization that we were asset rich, but cash poor. Our hyper-focus on planning for the future had put a lot of financial pressure on trying to live day to day, feeling really strained to enjoy life. I thought, "There must be something else. There must be another way!" I believed there had to be something out there, that I just hadn't discovered yet, a tool or idea that would help me build a financial bridge to live the vibrant life I dreamed of while also responsibly planning. How could we make a trip to Italy a reality for us? Because, even though we were doing all the right things, we felt discouraged that we didn't feel like we could enjoy the money we were making, and weren't getting ahead in significant ways, despite having good investments and good income.

Then 2008 hit. While the market crashed and the housing bubble burst, as a mom of three young kids, I held my head in my hands and wondered how the entire financial future my husband and I had built had been rocked, crumbling before our very eyes. More than just figuring it out for me and my hubby, I wanted certainty for my kids - my hubby and I desired to help them in every way. We wanted to set them up for as much success as possible, so that whatever they were put on the planet to do, they would be empowered to do it without the financial stress or worry that we had faced.

Today in this world, it can be hard to get ahead if you don't have support from your parents or some kind of inheritance. We wanted our kids to have every advantage to help them succeed, to live fully expressed in their own potential without restraint. Holding my head in my hands, I asked myself, "Is anything certain? What can I count on?"

BUILDING A BRIDGE

I realized that having a high income was quite different than creating lasting wealth. I decided it was up to me to discover what was working every time, all the time, regardless of what was happening in the economy around me. The financial crash of 2008 rocked my stability and freedom; Cinque Terre seemed even further away as we scrambled to understand our financial future in a market that was tanking.

We were so busy chasing rates of return, being conditioned to believe that much of our financial success was outside of our control. 2008 proved that for us. At this moment, I began searching for a better future for my family financially. I knew there had to be a better way than succumbing to the turbulence of typical financial planning. We had put all of our eggs in one basket, and it was time to switch things up.

The surprising truth is that the most important aspects of thriving financially are quite simple and completely under our control. Seeking safe and proven alternatives beyond the financial system status quo, an economist friend suggested I read a book called *Becoming Your Own Banker*. I filled its short 86 pages with highlighter, scribbled notes, and folded corners, opening my mind to new possibilities. I thought it was definitely something worthwhile, but it sounded too good to be true. And I wondered, "What's the catch?"

At the time, I didn't know it would guide me to helping families to be as prepared as possible, in moments they can't prepare for. When I picked up the book, I was simply looking for solutions to our own financial question marks. Looking back, I now know that my life's journey guided me in discovering how to build a financial foundation that fully supports my family, and the families I work with, to live abundantly and fully expressed!

This opened my mind to the world of using Dividend-Paying Whole Life Insurance and the Infinite Banking Concept. The skeptic in me put the book on a shelf for six months. One day my economist friend called and asked, "Hey Shalaree, did you want to do Infinite Banking?" For some reason, I was inspired to say YES.

That YES turned into buying my first whole life insurance policy for $20,000. It was time to test the water in a new way. I had $12,000 in property taxes for rental units that I needed to pay. For the first time, I was curious how I could do this without separating myself from my cash. I leveraged the policy to take a loan and borrow from the life insurance company to pay the property tax. I was diving in slowly but surely, testing the waters on what my money could truly do for my goals.

Having previously been a "pay cash" gal, I was fearful of having a loan. And although I had complete freedom and control over the payback without pressure, I diligently paid back the life insurance loan at $1,000/month, having it paid back within a year. I was relieved and surprised when this leap of faith worked in my favor. The system truly did provide the guarantees it said it would, and the liquid cash as promised. I needed to know more, not just for my family but for the countless middle class families who had been denied financial literacy on whole life insurance.

I dove all in. Shortly after, I traveled to Arizona to meet with an orthodontist and orthopedic surgeon who were teaching about how they were using whole life insurance to pay for operatories in their businesses, for their kids to go to college, take vacations, and more. As I immersed myself, I knew it was time to share this wisdom with other families and founders who wanted to grow their wealth for future generations while still enjoying their life today.

The dramatic clarity I discovered with finances activated in me a mission to teach families to be as prepared as possible, so they don't have to delay dreams or live with regrets, and can enjoy the vibrant freedom to live fully expressed. In 2013, I became a licensed life insurance provider. This step in my career has allowed me to live a life of abundance in all areas—spiritually, personally, with family and relationships, in purpose/career, and in finances. It sounds radical, but I actually solved my finances by educating myself and bringing financial awareness to my life, understanding what the wealthy were doing, and letting that be a solution for my family.

Now, I was able to help countless families do the same . . . opening their eyes to proven assets that are over 150 years old, and strategies used by most CEOs and executives. While the average worker has taken on all the risk by chasing rates of return with a qualified plan, executives get paid their bonuses with guaranteed assets like dividend-paying whole life insurance.

What I discovered was a bridge of freedom that allowed us to plan for the future with certainty and guarantees, while living happily and abundantly now.

. . . A bridge that took us from feeling asset rich and cash poor, to having access to liquid cash at any time, for any reason, without asking permission from anyone, giving us peace of mind and clarity to handle any surprise—an emergency or an opportunity— that will inevitably come.

. . . A bridge that took us from postponing our dreams of hiking Cinque Terre, Italy, to traveling internationally every other year, making priceless memories with our children.

FREEDOM TO LIVE FULLY EXPRESSED

Do you remember when I delayed hiking in Italy for 10 years? That was before I learned how to think differently and harness the power of my money in a way that worked for my family. Perhaps you've wondered what life looks when you don't fear every twist and turn of the stock market. Let me show you.

Late 2018, sitting at sushi dinner, my friend Tami said, "We want you and your family to go with us to Asia for my birthday." I was so excited, and yet also curious; how much would this cost?

These thoughts simultaneously ran through my brain... 'We didn't budget or plan for this trip. However, we've tried for years to vacation with these friends but our schedules never aligned.'

Then my husband reminded me that our kids were almost out of high school, so we may never have this chance again.

I considered it for a moment, then elatedly said, "We'd love to go to Asia!" How could I decide so quickly, effortlessly, and confidently?

The financial decisions I had made in the years after 2008 meant that in 2018 I didn't have to scrape out access to money that was locked up in assets. We had a model where we could pay back our Asia trip on our own timeline and on our own terms, while our money was still growing. The full amount of our cash value would continue to grow and compound inside our whole life insurance, *even if we leveraged some of it to go on vacation*, so going on the trip would not interrupt the growth of our money. We had certainty in our foundation for the future, so we were completely comfortable to travel and to celebrate when the opportunity came.

This is the independence and freedom our family gained with a change in thinking, creating a beautiful relationship with our finances, embracing the guarantees and Living Benefits of dividend-paying whole life insurance. Imagine what it would be like to have this same certainty and freedom to control the things that make your life more meaningful, so you can live a life that is deeply aligned and fully expressed.

LIVE YOUR LEGACY. LOVE YOUR WHOLE LIFE.

So what can owning dividend-paying whole life insurance as a financial bridge actually look like?

Before discovering whole life insurance, I would have paid $25,000 cash to go on vacation to Asia, which actually would have cost us $140,413 because we would have given up the growth we *could have made* on that money if we paid cash. By leveraging the cash value inside my whole life insurance, I kept our dollars growing uninterrupted and came out ahead an extra $160,082 over my lifetime. This is from *one vacation!* And this is without working any harder, or taking any additional risk. Imagine creating a financial bridge that allows you the freedom and control to finance big purchases differently.

Before discovering the power of whole life insurance, we paid cash for cars because it's obviously better than paying interest to someone else. I simply didn't understand the cost of paying cash. How many vehicles will you and your family buy in a lifetime? The average person buys nine vehicles. *NINE* ... think you, your partner, your spouse, your kids, your business. And all that money is gone if you pay cash or get a car loan from a bank, keeping you in a Save & Spend cycle.

In 2019 I bought my white Volvo, with white leather seats and the assisted parallel parking feature that I adore! If I had paid $42,000 cash, it would have actually cost me $235,894 because the money left me and could no longer grow. But by leveraging the cash value inside my whole life insurance, my dollars kept growing for life. I came out ahead $268,323 over my lifetime, without additional work or risk. How would an extra $268,000 of accessible tax-advantaged money sound when you want to stop working? I haven't even mentioned the additional millions of tax-free legacy simply by shifting:

1. our thinking
2. where we hold accessible cash reserves
3. how we finance the things we are already going to buy, recapturing dollars that would have been invisibly and silently lost.

There is *so much* that is completely under our control to get ahead and prosper, just by shifting how we think about money. Imagine being in a better financial position every year without working any harder, or taking any additional risk, simply by being more strategic about how you hold your savings dollars, and financing the things *you are going to purchase anyway* . . . it feels really good! This is one of the components behind the concept of Infinite Banking, of which I am a Certified and Authorized Practitioner.

Although I've shared everyday personal purchases like vehicles and vacations, the fact is, that when you pair whole life insurance and the Infinite Banking process, with cash-flowing investments like real estate or hard-money lending, the sky is the limit!

No matter how great your money is already working for you, imagine experiencing the full certainty and control that is truly possible! My heart is happy and peaceful because this is life insurance, guaranteed for my entire life, so we have the added bonus of protecting the family I love, knowing that when I'm gone—whether that's in five days, five months, five years or five decades—my family is taken care of.

IT'S NOT COMPLICATED

We have been taught to hand over part of our income for 20, 30, or 40 years and hope someone else knows what they're doing with our money better than we do. If you sent your kids off to boarding school for 15 years, would you have the same relationship as if you tucked them in and read books every night? Of course not! This is about a beautiful relationship unfolding with *your* money. You can feel empowered to know there are certainty and guarantees for you, so that your foundation doesn't crumble when the unexpected occurs.

THIS IS ABOUT NOT HAVING TO CHOOSE BETWEEN PREPARATION FOR THE FUTURE, AND BEING ABLE TO EXPERIENCE, RELISH, AND CHERISH LIFE ALONG THE WAY. THIS IS ABOUT BEING ABLE TO SAY "I KNOW," INSTEAD OF "I THINK" OR "I HOPE." AND LET ME TELL YOU, "I KNOW" IS A POWERFUL PLACE TO BE.

LESSONS LEARNED IN ASIA

Do you know what 100 Baht is worth? It seemed that's what every item cost in Thailand. 100 Baht (about $3.00 US)

Since riding an elephant was, of course, on the must-do list, our driver dropped us at a local place on the side of the road. Smiling, shoeless children ran about with dusty feet, adults quickly greeting us. Climbing up the wooden platform and onto the elephant, my view extended beyond the trees as our elephant lumbered amongst metal-sheeted huts and playful chickens.

I assumed the metal huts were storage, but seeing clothing hanging in one, and children in another, I eventually realized that the elephant path wandered amongst the residence of the families who owned the elephants. This path was their backyard; the elephants were an integral part of their livelihood and families. As we stopped for the obligatory photo, the driver pulled out a handful of small black circles.

Despite a clear language barrier, we finally discovered that the rings had been woven by the man, using tail hair from our elephant. The price for my new treasure? 100 Baht.

I silently marveled. Committed to caring for his animals and family using whatever resources available, this man had created jewelry from a strand of elephant tail-hair to help him live fully expressed.

The rest of the elephant ride back to the wooden platform was occupied by my thoughts: Did I fully appreciate my current resources and the abundance now available to me? Had I taken the same care and intentionality with my life, and for those I serve? Have I maximized the benefits of every dollar that I've earned or been blessed with?

I felt renewed with gratitude for the financial knowledge that has allowed the people I love most to live fully expressed in making memories we cherish traveling the world, fully expressed in confidence for our finances both now and in the future, and fully expressed in our love for each other, the dreams we have for impact in our lives, in our communities, and the world . . . deeply inspired that we each can make a difference in our own way. The black elephant hair ring is one of my most prized keepsakes from traveling through Asia, and I often think of that man, his family, and their elephant.

A LIFE OF FREEDOM, SIGNIFICANCE, & CERTAINTY: WHERE WE ARE NOW

Remember my little two-year-old who watched the Rick Steves' travel show about Cinque Terre? She is now almost a doctor, heading toward being a surgeon. She recently volunteered at a medical clinic serving the unhoused in Italy. She is a world traveler in her own right. Her younger sister will graduate next year with her Masters degree in prosthetics and orthotics, passionately empowering amputees to live fully expressed with mobility, eager to work with international non-profits who provide limbs to the underserved, and planning to open her own clinic one day. Both will have graduated without debt, living financially free to pursue their dreams, expressing their God-given passions and talents. And our youngest? Their brother is playing NCAA men's water polo, having the time of his life while working at an upscale restaurant, pursuing an economic degree on his way to law school, and having just partnered with me in his first real estate investment property, using our whole life insurance to help finance it. Truly for me, there is nothing that beats the satisfaction of helping your adult children live fully and freely, and watching them thrive!

STAY CURIOUS

Did you even know such a thing was possible with your money? Are you curious to build a beautiful working relationship with your money, and a financial future grounded in certainty and guarantees? Seek out a specialist—not someone who just sells insurance.

Work with someone you enjoy, who shares your values, and who is using dividend-paying whole life insurance as an *integral* part of their wealth building strategies. Seek out a certified and authorized Infinite Banking Practitioner. You don't want someone who is selling a product. You want a mentor for life that can fully support the abundance you deserve now and your family deserves for generations.

I believe dividend-paying whole life insurance is the most misunderstood asset. Don't miss out on its power and potential to support you with a rock solid financial foundation that can be part of a plan to give you incredible certainty, control, and confidence.

Whole life insurance has steadfastly survived and thrived during two World Wars, the Great Depression, and every uncertain economic event in between. You deserve the maximum benefits for your money. You deserve to have access, to know and understand the power of your dollars. The people you love and care for deserve to be protected. You deserve to enjoy the certainty that guarantees bring. You deserve the freedom to live a life that is fully expressed!

I am a financial professional, but not necessarily your financial professional. Everything in this chapter is for educational and entertainment purposes only. Here's to you living Financially Fully Expressed!

There are four important financial questions you must answer to build lasting wealth. Take some time to reflect on your current situation:

1. <u>Do you know your *"Freedom Number*?"</u> Your Freedom Number is how much you need in passive cash flow to live without working. Take your current annual expenses (you can guesstimate or get as detailed as you wish). Take your annual expenses divided by 12 months. This is your monthly Minimum Freedom Number, to make work optional. By having income produced from your assets, business automations, or anything that doesn't require you to actively make the money, you can experience more freedom in life. This is a great number to know. It's the 'why' that will guide your investing strategies, which is unique to each family and individual. This can often happen quicker when you focus on cash flow over accumulation. Find a qualified and experienced mentor in any investment strategy you pursue.

   Let's think abundantly! Want to know your Infinite Freedom Number? Take your Minimum Freedom Number and multiply it ... by any number: 2, 5, 10, or any number, *you choose the multiple.* In your wildest dreams, what would you do? Who would you spend time with? Where would you travel? What causes and organizations do you love and care about? With whom would you volunteer? What would you learn? How would you expand your life if money weren't an issue? Paint a picture of your dream life, write it down. Then write down your Infinite Freedom Number so you can set a subconscious goal right now.

2. <u>Do you know how much you should be *saving* to support your Freedom Number</u>? Savings is meant to save you in times of need, and to allow for opportunities of growth. Savings creates cash reserves. No matter how well your investments are doing, it's equally important to have money that is liquid and accessible and is never at risk. A great goal is to save at least 10% of your income. Many strong savers keep up to 20% or more of their income by paying themselves first.

3. <u>Do you know how much you should be *holding* in cash reserves to guarantee your protection and allow for opportunities</u>? The average business has about 27 days of liquidity. The average household has about the same amount. Why does this matter? If you feel financial pressure, it is likely reflecting how much liquidity you have, how much financial runway you have. Think about the values of certainty and uncertainty. We crave the thrill of uncertainty. That's why we ride roller coasters. But a roller coaster is only fun because we have the *certainty* of a seatbelt. A financial foundation of liquidity is the seatbelt that takes the financial pressure and stress out of the wild and exciting roller coaster of life.

4. <u>Do you know if where you hold money is *maximizing the benefits* you deserve</u>? Start thinking how you can give multiple jobs to one dollar, so your money is working harder than you do. With an environment that maximizes your benefits, you can take permanent ownership of your money, and harness the full potential of every dollar.

SHALAREE LAMBOY

LIFE INSURANCE PROFESSIONAL, AUTHORIZED PRACTITIONER OF THE INFINITE BANKING CONCEPT, WEALTH STRATEGIST

Shalaree Lamboy, a wealth strategist for Factum Financial, teaches pillars of foundational wealth to families and founders. Shalaree empowers women with a better way to control cash reserves, so they can reduce financial pressure and enjoy the certainty and confidence that comes from creating significant legacy, impact, and protection.

Shalaree has been a licensed life insurance professional for over a decade, and is an Authorized Practitioner of the Infinite Banking Concept, taught by the Nelson Nash Institute, a non-profit financial education company committed to teaching North Americans how to build wealth on firm principles that have stood the test of time.

shalareelamboy.com + www.FactumFoundations.com/Freedom
Instagram: @shalaree_lamboy

ELEVEN

A SUBCONSCIOUS NUDGE: THE QUIET POWER OF TUNING INTO YOUR INNER VOICE

JULIE COSTA

What if being fully expressed isn't about loud declarations, grand gestures, or social broadcasting? What if it's about tuning into your own voice and having the courage to hear it, even when it feels quiet, subtle, or different from what others expect? True expression comes not from conforming to the world's expectations but from the deep, authentic connection to ourselves. It is a practice of discerning the messages of our bodies, our hearts, and our intuition and allowing them to guide us in ways that are aligned with our deepest truth.

In a world that is increasingly emotionally charged, the ability to feel safe, grounded, and at peace within yourself is paramount. It is the difference between using your intuition to guide where you focus your energy and spending your days emptying your emotional cup before 10 a.m. There is a quiet power in choosing when, where, and how you express yourself. Learning to trust your own voice and allow that inner wisdom to shape your actions is an ongoing practice. This requires intention, patience, and an unwavering commitment to self-awareness.

THE STRUGGLE WITH FINDING MY VOICE

Growing up, I never truly had the space to express myself. Raised by my dad after my mom unexpectedly passed, I often found myself holding back, my needs and emotions muted in the background. There were moments when I needed comfort, support, or just a simple act of care, but it wasn't always available. The dynamic was such that I wasn't able to share my feelings or even recognize them fully.

In this silence, I began to learn that expression, true expression, was more than just communicating your thoughts or desires to others. It was a form of self-affirmation. But this became difficult for me because, in many ways, I didn't even know how to articulate what I needed. I wasn't encouraged to speak up. It wasn't that my dad didn't love me, but he didn't always know how to provide the space for me to express my emotions. And so, I learned to live in a quiet place, hiding parts of myself that I thought were unworthy of being seen.

For years, I lived in this quiet conflict, torn between the voice I had yet to discover and the world around me that demanded I conform. This struggle followed me into adulthood. I felt like an outsider, out of sync with the world and my own needs. The more

I pushed those needs down, the harder it became to find a way out. But that all changed when I started practicing hypnotherapy and subconscious reprogramming.

A SUBCONSCIOUS NUDGE TOWARD CHANGE

My journey into hypnotherapy was anything but conventional. It began in a dark place. I was emotionally drained, feeling stuck, and asking my late mother for a sign. It was in that moment of vulnerability and longing that I received a nudge, an unmistakable inner voice urging me to step into the world of hypnotherapy. This was a whisper from my subconscious, a call to action that, had I not been open to hearing it, might have passed me by.

I took that nudge seriously. At the time, I was at a low point emotionally, and I knew I needed a change. Little did I know that this decision would unlock a door to a deeper understanding of myself. Hypnotherapy taught me to tune into my body and heart's true alignment, rather than constantly seeking external validation. It was through this process that I learned to discern the difference between the noise of the outside world and the quiet voice within that was always trying to guide me.

Hypnotherapy wasn't just about accessing hidden memories or uncovering deep truths. It was about shedding the emotional charge that had been clouding my judgment for years. It was about recognizing that I had the power to decide what to express and when, instead of reacting to the pressure of external expectations.

THIS PRACTICE TAUGHT ME THAT TRUE
EXPRESSION IS AN INTERNAL PROCESS, IT'S
NOT ABOUT BROADCASTING FOR OTHERS,
BUT ABOUT ALIGNING WITH YOUR INNER
TRUTH AND ALLOWING YOUR ACTIONS TO
NATURALLY FOLLOW.

THE POWER OF DISCRETION IN EXPRESSION

One of the most valuable lessons I learned through this practice was the importance of discretion. Expression is not always about speaking your mind, especially when your inner voice is still finding its clarity. There is a quiet strength in knowing when to speak and when to listen. Sometimes, the best form of expression is simply being still and allowing yourself the space to think before acting.

This was especially evident during my 10-year career working at lululemon. I found myself in conflict with the company's values that they preached and what was really happening on the daily. Rather than continue to feel the tension internally, I expressed my frustration. It felt empowering in the moment, but ultimately, it led to me being fired. In hindsight, I realized that my expression, though valid, wasn't aligned with where I needed to be at that time. The rejection, however, was not a rejection, it was redirection. It allowed me to step away from an environment that wasn't in alignment with my deeper values and opened the door for me to pursue work that truly resonated with my authentic self.

The lesson here was clear: rejection can sometimes be the universe's way of helping you find your true path. Being fully expressed isn't about forcing yourself into situations where you don't belong, it's about recognizing when it's time to move on, when to speak your truth, and when to quietly listen.

THE IMPORTANCE OF INTERNAL PEACE

One of the key components of being fully expressed is cultivating a deep sense of internal peace. In today's world, with its constant flow of opinions, information, and external noise, it can be easy to feel overwhelmed by the expectations of others. But I've learned that it is essential to create space for yourself, to tune out the noise, and to reconnect with your own inner rhythm.

Living in alignment with your authentic self means acting from a place of inner peace, not external pressure. It's about listening to your own intuition, rather than being swayed by the ever-present influence of social media, podcasts, or the well-meaning advice of others. When you are connected to your own truth, you will find that your actions naturally align with your values, and you no longer feel the need to prove yourself to others.

This practice of tuning in and tuning out is crucial for staying grounded and present in your own life. It allows you to focus on what truly matters and express yourself in ways that are meaningful, not performative. Your actions speak louder than words, and when you are at peace with your choices, your expression becomes effortless.

IT'S OKAY TO NOT BE FULLY EXPRESSED RIGHT NOW

A crucial point to remember is that it's okay not to be fully expressed, especially in the early stages of your journey. Expression is a process, it evolves over time as you grow and change. It's natural to go through phases where you don't feel ready to speak up or share every part of yourself with the world. What matters is that you are moving toward a place where you can fully align with your truth.

Being fully expressed doesn't mean constantly broadcasting your thoughts or opinions. Sometimes, it means honoring the times when silence is the best expression. It's okay to feel unsure, to question, and to hold space for yourself as you navigate your own truth. As you build trust in yourself and your intuition, you'll find that the moments of expression will come naturally and will feel authentic, rather than forced.

THE QUIET STRENGTH OF BEING FULLY EXPRESSED

Ultimately, being fully expressed isn't about being loud or outwardly visible, it's about tuning into your inner voice, aligning with your truth, and acting from a place of peace and self-awareness. It's about recognizing that your worth doesn't come from the validation of others, but from the quiet knowing that you are living in alignment with your most authentic self.

In a world full of noise and distractions, there is immense power in choosing to listen, to tune out the chaos, and to create space for your own voice to rise. As you step into the quiet strength of being fully expressed, you will find that your actions naturally align with your inner truth, and you'll begin to experience a deeper sense of fulfillment and peace. Trust yourself, honor your intuition, and know that you are enough, just as you are.

In a world full of noise and distractions, there is immense power in choosing to listen, to tune out the chaos, and to create space for your own voice to rise. For me, that moment of quieting the noise came when I was consciously choosing to keep my full-time job for stability and security while I built my business. The demands were overwhelming. Balancing work, growing my business, and maintaining my personal life often felt like too much to manage. There were days when I was stretched thin, questioning how I could do it all.

In those moments, I turned to my tools for support, specifically a hypnosis audio that focused on trust and surrender. I realized that I was holding on tightly to control, trying to make everything happen on my own terms, and this only fueled the overwhelm. I needed to let go, step into peace, and learn to flow with life rather than fight against it. Each day, I would listen to the audio, reprogramming my beliefs around trust and surrender. It helped me release the stories that kept me stuck in control and allowed me to embrace the journey with more ease and grace. I started feeling more aligned, more at peace, and better able to handle the balance between my job and my growing business.

This practice of tuning out the chaos, whether through silence, focused audio, or simply quieting my mind became the foundation for finding my own inner truth. As I stepped into the quiet strength of being fully expressed, I found that my actions naturally aligned with my inner wisdom. I began to experience a deeper sense of fulfillment and peace, trusting that the steps I was taking, even when they felt small, were leading me exactly where I needed to go.

Trust yourself, honor your intuition, and know that you are enough, just as you are. If you've been feeling overwhelmed or struggling to let go of control, I invite you to try the same practice that helped me. I've created a Trust and Surrender audio bundle to help you reconnect with your inner voice, release the overwhelm, and step into the flow of life. Download the free bundle here and start your journey toward peace today.

Check out an exclusive HypnoBreathwork, Hypnosis + Subliminal Bundle: Trust & Surrender: https://www.juliemcosta.com/offers/J7HCcJto/checkout?coupon_code=FULLYEXPRESSED

ABOUT THE AUTHOR

JULIE COSTA

BUSINESS HYPNOTHERAPIST AND NLP TRAINER

Julie Costa is a business hypnotherapist & NLP trainer. She uses subconscious reprogramming to help business owners rewire their mind for success, smash limiting beliefs, and uplevel their money mindset both professionally and personally.

As both a coach for businesses across industries and the founder of ANCHORED, a board accredited certification program, Julie equips business owners and coaches with tools that cut through the noise, reprogram subconscious beliefs, and uplevel business success.

www.juliemcosta.com
Instagram: @julie.m.costa